KU-792-122

# THIS IS MALAYSIA

# THIS IS MALAYSIA

*Text by Wendy Moore*
*Photographs by Gerald Cubitt*

First published in the UK in 1995 by
New Holland (Publishers) Ltd
24 Nutford Place, London W1H 6DQ



ISBN 1 85368 375 2

Commissioning Editor: Tim Jollands
Editor: Beverley Jollands
Designer: Philip Mann, ACE Limited
Cartography: Julian Baker
Index: Beverley Jollands

Reproduction by HBM Print (Pte.) Ltd, Singapore
Printed and bound in Singapore by Tien Wah Press (Pte.) Ltd

# Contents

# Photographic Acknowledgements

The publishers extend their thanks to the following individuals and organizations who kindly loaned their photographs for inclusion in this book. All the photographs in the book, with the exception of those listed below, were taken by Gerald Cubitt.

Malaysia Tourism Promotion Board: page 131 (below)

Linda Pitkin: page 101 (below), page 138 (below right), page 139, pages 167 to 172

Raman Mohd. Noh: page 4, page 5, page 6, page 7, page 18, page 25, page 30 (left), page 35, page 37, page 71 (below), page 75 (above left), 78 (above), page 85 (below), page 102 (above right and below left), page 103, page 107 (above left and above right), page 108, page 109 (above), page 110 (above and below left), page 112 (above right and below), page 113 (below), page 115 (centre and below), page 117 (below), page 118, page 119, page 122, page 127 (below), page 129

Royal Geographical Society: page 10, page 11, page 13, page 14, page 16, page 20, page 27, page 29, page 32, page 36, page 39, page 40, page 45, page 48, page 50, page 52, page 56

Sabah Museum: page 31

Illustrations appearing in the preliminary pages are as follows:

HALF TITLE: Now an endangered species, the Tiger (*Felis tigris*) occurs in Peninsular Malaysia but not in Sabah and Sarawak.

FRONTISPIECE: Dipterocarp forest, the natural vegetation of Malaysia from coastal lowland to the interior hill ranges.

TITLE PAGE: Sunset over the South China Sea.

PAGE 4: A colourful shop-front in Kuala Terengganu.

PAGE 5: Drummers at Kelantan's annual drum festival playing *rebana*, giant drums made from hollowed logs.

PAGE 7: Sungai Ular, one of the many traditional fishing communities lining the Peninsula's east coast.

BELOW: Built for a chieftain in 1894, Penghulu's House near Melaka is the perfect example of a traditional Malay house.

# ACKNOWLEDGEMENTS

The author, photographers and publishers would like
to express their gratitude to the following for their generous and valuable assistance during the preparation of this book:

MALAYSIA
Malaysia Tourism Promotion Board, Ministry of Culture, Arts & Tourism
Malaysia Airlines
The Director General, Department of Wildlife & National Parks
World Wide Fund for Nature (WWF) Malaysia
The Director General, Forest Research Institute, Malaysia
Malayan Nature Society
National Parks & Wildlife Office, Sarawak Forestry Department
Ministry of Tourism & Environmental Development: Sabah Wildlife Department
Shangri-La Hotels, Kuala Lumpur and Penang (Golden Sands)
Eastern & Oriental Express
Mohd. Khan bin Momin Khan
Dr Salleh Mohd. Nor
Susan Abraham
Dr Kiew Bong Heang
Dr Tho Yow Pong
Heah Hock Heang
Philip Ngau Jalong
Dr Elizabeth Bennett
David Labang
Francis Liew
Dr Clive Marsh
Tony and Anthea Lamb
Dr Rob Steubing
Rosemarie Wee
Victor and Micky Smete

SINGAPORE
Peter Ng, Singapore University

GREAT BRITAIN
The trustees and staff of the Natural History Museum, London
Dr John Dransfield, Royal Botanic Gardens, Kew
Dr Roy Watling, Royal Botanic Garden, Edinburgh
Dr George Argent, Royal Botanic Garden, Edinburgh
Rosemary Smith, Royal Botanic Garden, Edinburgh

Special thanks also go to:
Ken Scriven
Janet Cubitt
Jack Jackson
The Royal Geographical Society

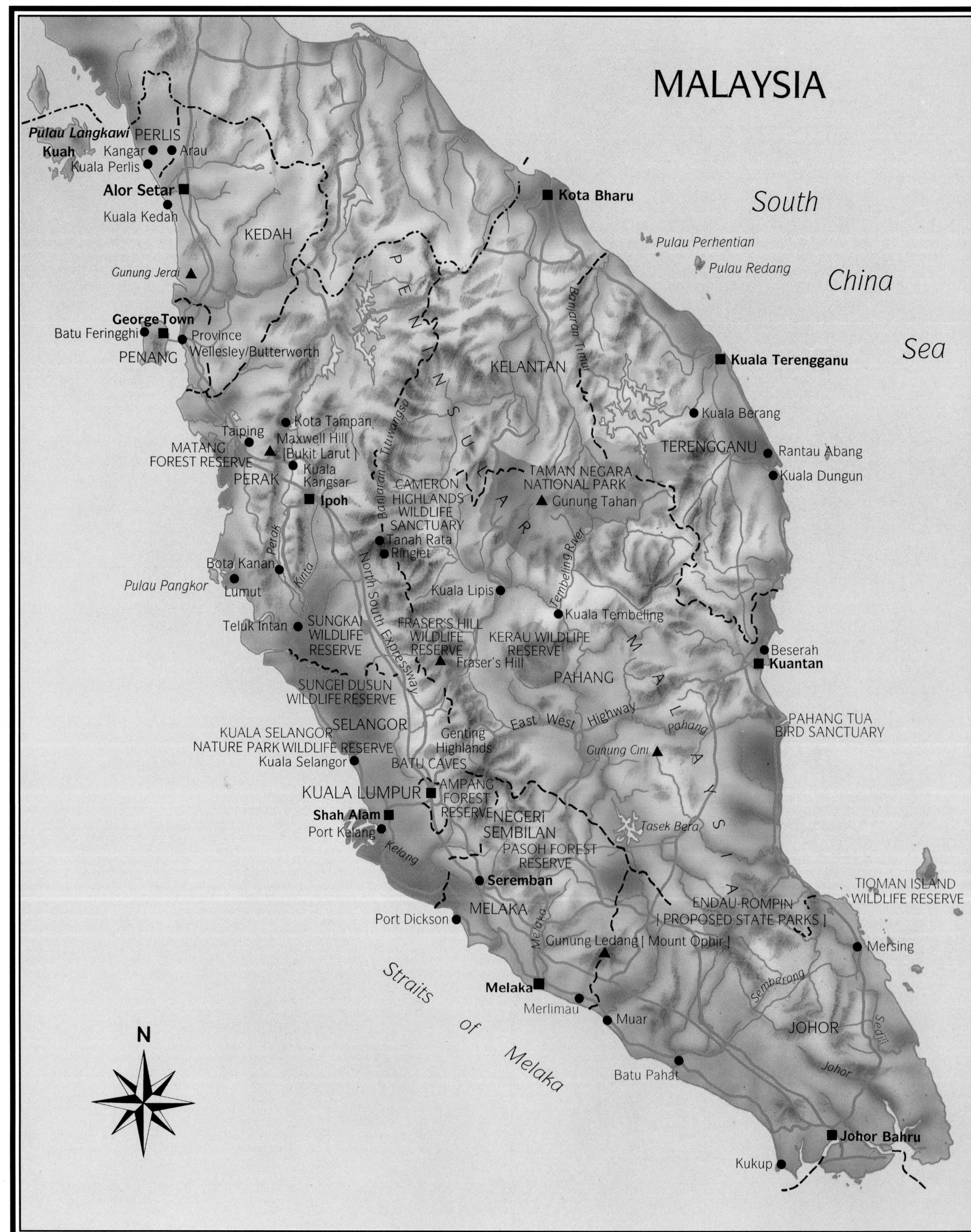
MALAYSIA
South China Sea
Straits of Melaka
N
Pulau Langkawi
Kuah
PERLIS
Kangar
Arau
Kuala Perlis
Alor Setar
Kuala Kedah
KEDAH
Gunung Jerai
George Town
Batu Feringghi
Province Wellesley/Butterworth
PENANG
Kota Bharu
Pulau Perhentian
Pulau Redang
Banjaran Timur
KELANTAN
Kuala Terengganu
Kuala Berang
TERENGGANU
Rantau Abang
Kuala Dungun
PENINSULAR MALAYSIA
Banjaran Titiwangsa
Kota Tampan
Taiping
Maxwell Hill [Bukit Larut]
MATANG FOREST RESERVE
Kuala Kangsar
PERAK
Ipoh
CAMERON HIGHLANDS WILDLIFE SANCTUARY
TAMAN NEGARA NATIONAL PARK
Gunung Tahan
Tembeling River
Tanah Rata
Ringlet
Perak
Kinta
Bota Kanan
Pulau Pangkor
Lumut
Kuala Lipis
Kuala Tembeling
North South Expressway
Teluk Intan
SUNGKAI WILDLIFE RESERVE
FRASER'S HILL WILDLIFE RESERVE
Fraser's Hill
KERAU WILDLIFE RESERVE
PAHANG
Beserah
Kuantan
SUNGEI DUSUN WILDLIFE RESERVE
SELANGOR
KUALA SELANGOR NATURE PARK WILDLIFE RESERVE
Kuala Selangor
Genting Highlands
BATU CAVES
East West Highway
Pahang
PAHANG TUA BIRD SANCTUARY
Gunung Cini
KUALA LUMPUR
AMPANG FOREST RESERVE
Shah Alam
Port Kelang
Kelang
NEGERI SEMBILAN
PASOH FOREST RESERVE
Tasek Bera
Seremban
Port Dickson
MELAKA
Melaka
Gunung Ledang [ Mount Ophir ]
ENDAU-ROMPIN [ PROPOSED STATE PARKS ]
TIOMAN ISLAND WILDLIFE RESERVE
Mersing
Sembrong
Melaka
Merlimau
Muar
JOHOR
Sedili
Johor
Batu Pahat
Johor Bahru
Kukup

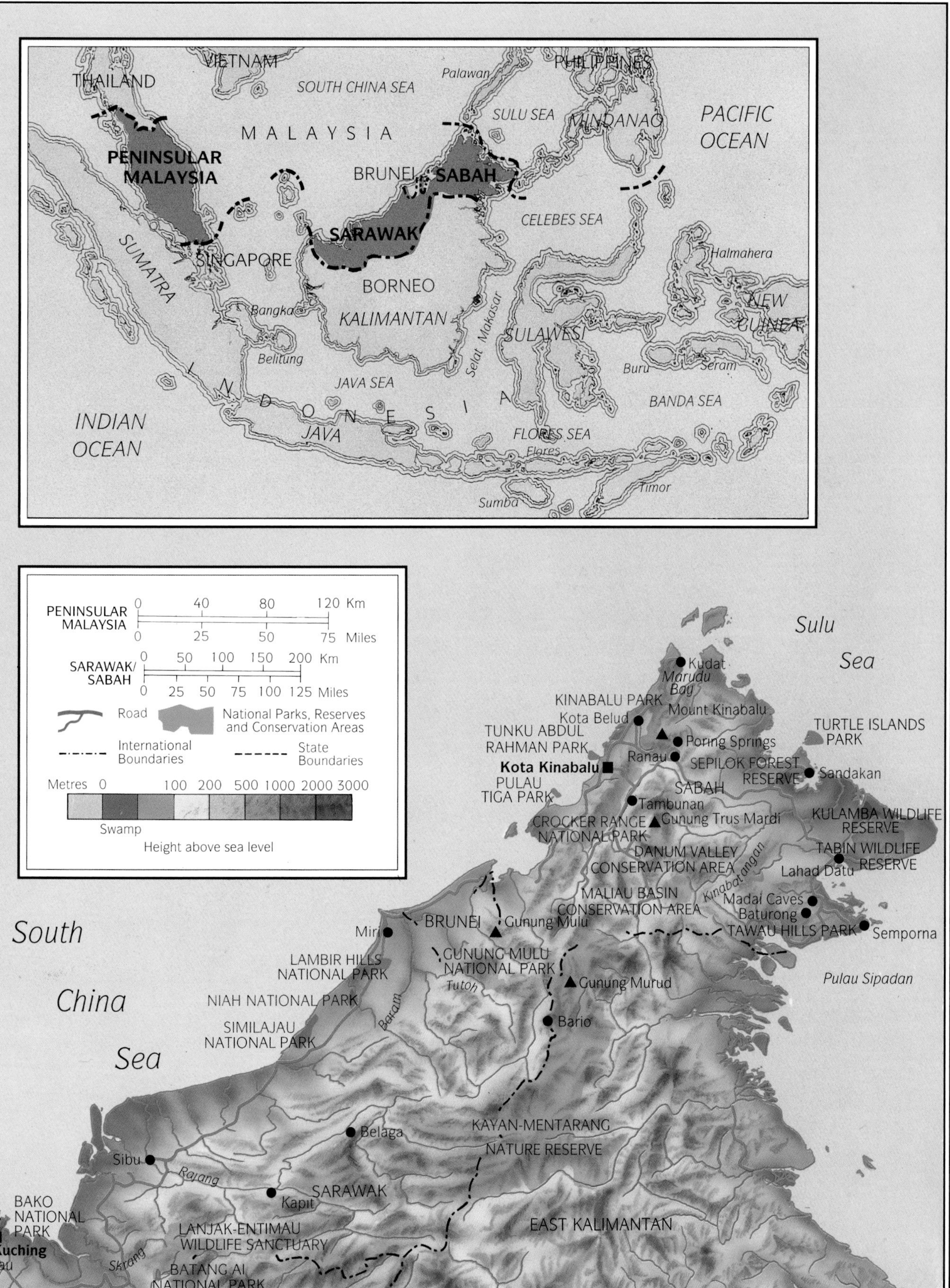
THAILAND
VIETNAM
SOUTH CHINA SEA
Palawan
PHILIPPINES
SULU SEA
MINDANAO
PACIFIC OCEAN
MALAYSIA
PENINSULAR MALAYSIA
BRUNEI
SABAH
SARAWAK
CELEBES SEA
SUMATRA
SINGAPORE
BORNEO
KALIMANTAN
Bangka
Belitung
Selat Makasar
SULAWESI
Halmahera
NEW GUINEA
Buru
Seram
JAVA SEA
INDONESIA
BANDA SEA
INDIAN OCEAN
JAVA
FLORES SEA
Flores
Timor
Sumba
PENINSULAR MALAYSIA
0 40 80 120 Km
0 25 50 75 Miles
SARAWAK/ SABAH
0 50 100 150 200 Km
0 25 50 75 100 125 Miles
Road
National Parks, Reserves and Conservation Areas
International Boundaries
State Boundaries
Metres 0 100 200 500 1000 2000 3000
Swamp
Height above sea level
Sulu Sea
Kudat
Marudu Bay
KINABALU PARK
Mount Kinabalu
Kota Belud
TURTLE ISLANDS PARK
TUNKU ABDUL RAHMAN PARK
Poring Springs
Ranau
Kota Kinabalu
SEPILOK FOREST RESERVE
Sandakan
PULAU TIGA PARK
SABAH
Tambunan
CROCKER RANGE NATIONAL PARK
Gunung Trus Madi
KULAMBA WILDLIFE RESERVE
DANUM VALLEY CONSERVATION AREA
TABIN WILDLIFE RESERVE
Lahad Datu
Kinabatangan
MALIAU BASIN CONSERVATION AREA
Madai Caves
Baturong
TAWAU HILLS PARK
Semporna
South China Sea
Miri
BRUNEI
Gunung Mulu
LAMBIR HILLS NATIONAL PARK
GUNUNG MULU NATIONAL PARK
Tutoh
Gunung Murud
Pulau Sipadan
NIAH NATIONAL PARK
Baram
Bario
SIMILAJAU NATIONAL PARK
KAYAN-MENTARANG NATURE RESERVE
Belaga
Sibu
Rajang
Kapit
SARAWAK
BAKO NATIONAL PARK
Santubong
Kuching
Bau
GUNUNG GADING NATIONAL PARK
LANJAK-ENTIMAU WILDLIFE SANCTUARY
EAST KALIMANTAN
Skrang
BATANG AI NATIONAL PARK
WEST KALIMANTAN

# PROFILE OF MALAYSIA

Descending from celestial heights the aircraft punches through a monsoonal cloud bank to reveal the South China Sea below, shimmering in a heat haze and edged to either horizon with a ribbon of beaches. Creeping out and merging with it, muddying its powder-blue waters, are the tentacles of an ochre river which snakes through the green lowlands, like the serpentine coils of stylized dragons on those great Shanghai jars so coveted by Borneo's indigenous tribes. A vast blanket of trees stretches away into the distance, looking from this bird's-eye vantage-point like a giant broccoli garden. Then around a bend in the river looms a gold-domed mosque, a sprawl of tin roofs, a couple of high-rise hotels, and scars of red earth recently bulldozed for plantations and suburbs. This is Malaysia.

Situated at the hub of South-east Asia, south of Thailand and north of Singapore and Indonesia, Malaysia embraces over 330,000 square kilometres (128,000 square miles) of tropical rainforests, palm-clad beaches, and rugged mountain ranges. It comprises the Malay Peninsula (formerly known as Malaya) – the southernmost extremity of the Asian mainland – together with the Bornean states of Sabah and Sarawak, often described as East Malaysia, which are partitioned from the peninsula by nearly 600 kilometres (370 miles) of the South China Sea.

In the 13th century, when Marco Polo made his celebrated sea voyage from China to India, he revealed a world almost totally unknown to western Christendom: a place of legendary kingdoms, weird creatures, exotic peoples and their fabulous riches. But while these realms were *terra incognita* for Europeans, the same sea-roads that the Venetian merchant sailed had been plied by Arab dhows and Chinese junks for centuries. These routes were the highways of antiquity while Europe was still slumbering in the Dark Ages.

Peninsular Malaysia was perfectly situated for maritime trade. The south-west winds blew the Indians and Arabs across the Bay of Bengal while the north-easterly monsoon filled the sails of Chinese junks *en route* to the Malay archipelago and the great island of Borneo. At its height, this maritime trade route – down the South China Sea, through the Straits of Melaka, into the Indian Ocean and thence to the Red Sea – was a second Silk Road. The legendary kingdom of Langkasuka, in the north-east of the peninsula, was famed for its camphor-wood, and traders came seeking rhinoceros horn and other jungle exotica collected by the nomads that roamed the towering rainforests of the interior.

Malaysia's name derives from its former title, Malaya, which in turn comes from the name of its dominant race, the Malays, and earlier still from the seventh-century kingdom of Melayu in Sumatra. Malay history, however, is usually regarded as beginning with the great trading kingdom of Melaka (previously spelt 'Malacca') which reached the zenith of its power in the 15th century.

PREVIOUS PAGES

Page 10, above left: *A member of Sarawak's largest indigenous group, this Iban girl's elaborate jewellery was wrought by Maloh silversmiths from West Kalimantan, with whom the Iban traded.*

Above right: *Shinning up a palm tree to pick coconuts on a Perak plantation, 1910.*

Below left: *A Bidayuh village near Kuching, Sarawak, in 1913. The Bidayuh are renowned bamboo-carvers, using it for everything from water-pipes to musical instruments.*

Below right: *Kuching, 1913: a Malay fisherwoman and her companion.*

Page 11: *Iban family heirlooms include brass gongs and huge Chinese jars used for storing rice and wine. Such treasures had traditional uses as currency and dowries.*

It was founded by the Sumatran prince Parameswara, whose impeccable pedigree, according to the court annals, *Sejarah Melayu*, could be traced back to Alexander the Great. Of all the ports on the ancient trade route, Melaka, 'Queen of the Spice Trade', was the most famed. The medieval sultans and their courtiers enjoyed a life of opulence, residing in gilded palaces, borne aloft on silk-caparisoned elephants and waited on by scores of slave girls. Melaka's importance to that era is obvious from a frequently quoted remark by the historian Tomé Pires after the Portuguese had successfully conquered the port in 1511; he wrote that the city was 'of such importance and profit that it seems to me it has no equal in the world'.

Today, Melaka is a thriving modern town, but it retains remnants of its celebrated past, as does Penang, 'the Pearl of the Orient'. However, these older centres are eclipsed by Kuala Lumpur, the colonial capital of the British imperialists, which has easily outstripped its rivals to become Malaysia's fastest-growing city. Remarkably, despite its changing skyline, Kuala Lumpur still boasts some splendid Moorish buildings from the colonial era.

It is said that in Melaka's heyday more than 80 different languages were spoken in its streets, as traders from dozens of different nations and from the far-flung corners of the known world converged at the famed entrepôt. These days, Malaysia's population of 18 million may not speak quite so many dialects, but Melaka laid the groundwork for the multiracial and multicultural nature of the modern nation. Malays, Orang Asli, Ibans, Kadazans, and dozens of other indigenous groups live harmoniously side by side with later immigrant peoples like the Chinese, Indians and Eurasians. This variegated mix of cultures is one of Malaysia's biggest drawcards, for apart from the fascination of finding mosques, temples and churches in the same streets, the calendar is crammed with festivities, and Malaysian cuisine offers the best of Malay, Chinese and Indian dishes.

On the Peninsula, the east coast is more obviously Malay in character than the west, which took the brunt of the massive 19th-century immigrations. In timeless fishing villages, arts and crafts survive and traditional performances are still popular, although western culture has certainly made inroads here as it has everywhere. The average Malaysian family now owns its own car, and even the most upriver longhouses boast television sets, but the *adat*, or tradition, which was ingrained here even before Islam arrived in the 14th century, is still just as strong.

On the other side of the South China Sea, in the states of Sarawak and Sabah, the population is as mosaic as the Peninsula's, but the Bornean myths created in the heyday of the British empire are still a potent force in luring visitors to their shores. In Victorian days, British armchair travellers were enthralled by tales in the illustrated weeklies which told of a great jungled isle, peopled with head-hunters, pirates and Orang-utans. Tales of the exploits of James Brooke, an adventurous Englishman who had been rewarded with a large chunk of Borneo for helping the Raja Muda of Brunei suppress an uprising, made front-page news back in England. Brooke's exploits against the Dayak head-hunters, and tales of the weird and wonderful creatures in his domain, made for compelling reading. The tattooed tribesmen, pictured in hornbill-feather head-dresses, some with pendulous earlobes, were portrayed as though they spent their entire adult lives collecting human heads. Of course nothing could be further from the truth, but these were the tales on which the mythical Borneo was built, and which to a certain extent still linger today.

As in developing nations the world over, many traditional lifestyles have changed forever in the wake of progress, but East Malaysia is still one of the world's last frontiers. Out of sight of the oil-boom towns and logging camps it is not too difficult to find the old Borneo, where rivers still run free amid the world's oldest rainforests.

When Isabella Bird, the celebrated Victorian authoress, journeyed into the Malay Peninsula in 1879 there were few roads and no tourists; cross-country travel was accomplished on elephant-back. But when Cuthbert Woodville Harrison wrote his *Guide to Malaya* in 1923 he remarked that 'Even Malaya, the land of the kris, the piratical prahu, and the bloody and treacherous Malayan people . . . has now become a quiet middle of the world'. He added that this might be regretted by some, but to most people, and particularly those who live here, 'it is matter for very profound satisfaction. Over one thousand miles of railway and two thousand five hundred miles of road deal shrewd blows at romance . . .'.

The changes that the colonial era produced were summed up by Henri Fauconnier, the French planter turned prize-winning author who remarked: 'Between the Malaya of my youth, and the Malaya of today there is as much difference as between Gaul before the Roman conquest and France as we know it. In twenty years I have seen this country make good a delay of twenty centuries.'

Malaysia today is one of the 'tiger' economies of South-east Asia. Most villages now have access to electricity and piped water, and unemployment is at an all-time low. Motor vehicles clog the nation's roads and contribute to ever increasing pollution, while forests are being denuded and wetlands drained. But the population is healthier, better fed and housed than in the past, and there are few who laud the past over the present. And, for all these changes, there are still huge tracts of undisturbed rainforest, idyllic tropical islands, deserted beaches, superb colonial architecture, cool highland resorts, and the added advantage of a diverse and hospitable population.

## THE LAND

It is mid-afternoon and the hothouse land lies listless in a tropical torpor, waiting for the expected downpour. A navy-blue thunderhead climbs ominously overhead at Taiping, the Peninsula's wettest town, where the coffee-shops are in a flurry of activity as patrons wait to see exactly when the rain will start, having earlier in the day placed their bets on the timing of the afternoon shower.

Arching across the road at the town's Lake Gardens, forming a cathedral-like canopy, are huge, century-old rain-trees. Their branches are each as large as an average tree trunk and every nook and cranny is festooned with Bird's Nest Ferns, bunches of Fish-bone Ferns and at least 15 other fern species, not to mention the wispy creepers, the mosses that daub the bark like an artist's palette, and orchids with their translucent alabaster-hued flowers: testimony to the town's prolific rainfall.

*A palm oil mill in Penang, 1899. From such small beginnings Malaysia has become the world's largest producer of palm oil.*

At precisely 3.45pm the palms sway crazily, their fronds clattering in the gusts that always pre-empt a tropical thunderstorm. Then the heavens open and the life-giving rain pounds the earth, nurturing, nourishing, and bathing the land anew. Debts are settled and winnings are pocketed at the coffee-shops while the customers settle back to sip their drinks and wait for the rain to ease. No one attempts to venture out, for the sheer volume of water can saturate clothes in seconds.

In Malaysia, as in most equatorial countries, the rain is not a gentle watering but a deluge. A resort proprietor in Pahang's Pulau Tioman was bemused when a German guest ran outside during the afternoon shower and stared transfixed at the sky – he had never before seen rain in such volume. But it is evident from the incredible lushness of Malaysia's landscape, where green is the predominant shade, that to sustain such verdant growth the rainfall must be abundant. One only has to look at the size of the stormwater drains beside every road to be in no further doubt.

The sombre halls of the great vaulted rainforests, the endless plantations of rubber trees and oil palms, the shimmering rice-fields, the inhospitable, but important, wetlands, the life cycles of flowers, plants and the prolific wildlife, not to mention the farmers and fishermen and other agriculturists – all of these depend for their livelihood on the rain. However, Malaysia differs from other rainforest regions like the Congo and the Amazon, which rely on uniform rainfall, as it is ultimately dependent on the regime of the annual monsoons, or *musim*, a word of Arabic origin which is still used by the Malays to denote the seasons. Ancient mariners knew Peninsular Malaysia as 'The Land Where the Winds Meet', as this thin strip of land jutting from the bottom of Asia was a natural stopover for sailing ships awaiting the change of winds from the north-east to the south-west monsoon, or vice versa. Known as the *musim tutup kuala*, the 'season when the estuaries close', the north-east monsoon which blows from November to April dumps the bulk of its watery load on the east coast of the Peninsula and on Sabah and Sarawak. Flooding is frequent and is often a yearly event for folk living in low-lying areas. The monsoon is the time to fix boats and nets, and wait out its yearly wrath on shore.

*The Pahang River, the longest river in Peninsular Malaysia, at Pekan, the former royal capital of Pahang, in about 1890.*

Sometimes it can rain for weeks on end – an ordeal which can try the patience of even the most easygoing inhabitant. Once in the 1930s, Kelantan experienced 29 solid days of rain. Patrick Balfour recorded the event in his 1935 novel *Grand Tour*, in which that saturated month broke the spirit of a young English bride whose visit coincided with the downpour. Her trousseau mildewed and she was house-bound for a month. Her introduction to the East could not have been worse, but there was a twist. Before her arrival it had been said that she would wear the trousers in the household, but the monsoon fixed that. As Balfour recounted: 'It is said by some that Prentice arranged on purpose to be married at the beginning of the rains. Even so, he could have hardly foreseen that a record rainfall would play so neatly into his hands.'

Situated between one and seven degrees north of the equator, Malaysia is hot and humid all year round. Temperature variations throughout the year are slight and the mercury usually hovers between 22° and 32℃ (72° and 90℉). A glance at the nightly television weather forecast says it all; the temperature for Kuala Lumpur is always between 30° and 33℃ (86° and 91℉), which explains why many Malaysians find the daily weather report so boring. The humidity is always high and readings of 98 per cent are not uncommon. Baking in a concrete overcoat, Kuala Lumpur and, to a lesser extent, the other cities always retain the heat of the day much more than in the countryside. Awakening in a *kampung*, the traditional Malay hamlet, when the dew is still on the grass and the air is cool and fresh, is a delightful experience compared to the torpid city heat or the dry, artificial environment of an air-conditioned room.

To escape the stifling heat, the colonialists built hill retreats like Cameron Highlands and Fraser's Hill, where at elevations of over 1,800 metres (6,000 feet) the temperature is considerably cooler. The mercury drops even more on lofty Mount Kinabalu in Sabah: at the overnight stop on the summit trail, the temperature range is a mere 2° to 10℃ (36° to 50℉). Pools of water ice over, and hail is not uncommon. Hugh Low, the first European to try to climb the peak in 1851, was told by the native Kadazans before his ascent that on the summit a dragon guarded an immense jewel and that strewn around were enormous grey pearls that no man dared touch, for to do so would flood the world below. Scholars suppose that these pearls were actually hailstones, which fall only in the higher altitudes. Rarely, hailstorms occur in the lowlands, but they are such an uncommon event that during a recent storm, the children in a Johor *kampung* ran about excitedly calling out '*salji*,' the Malay word for 'snow' taken from the Arabic, while the older women, some of whom had never seen hail before, muttered the Islamic incantation to drive away the devil.

Back in the primeval dawn of time the Malay Peninsula was not separated from Borneo by hundreds of kilometres of sea, but was joined in a great land mass known as Sundaland which encompassed not only present-day Malaysia but the other islands of the Malay Archipelago including Java and Sumatra. Elephants, rhinoceroses, monkeys, Orang-utans, deer, and hundreds of other species both great and small trooped across this terrestrial bridge, but when the Ice Age ended and the waters which had been locked up in ice rose once more, the lowlands flooded and Borneo was left to evolve in isolation. The ancient land bridges explain why so many species throughout the region are so similar. Malaysia did not suffer from the cataclysmic climate changes of the Ice Age to the same extent as Africa and South America, which explains why the South-east Asian rainforests are of such antiquity. Of all the forests of this region, Malaysia's have been the least disturbed, for they have experienced no volcanic eruptions, typhoons or earthquakes to upset their equilibrium, unlike those of the Philippines, Java and Sumatra.

The forests of Malaysia remained virtually untouched until relatively recently, when humans, the despoilers, came upon the scene. Before the British colonialists began their drive into the Peninsula's hinterland in the late 19th century Malaysia's rainforests grew undisturbed, fringing the Malay coastal settlements, swathing the lowlands of the west coast, over the mountainous granite backbone of the Banjaran Titiwangsa, across the hills of the interior, and practically to the beaches of the east coast. What an awesome sight these forests must have been, stretching unbroken from the border of Thailand in the north, blanketing the Peninsula for 740 kilometres (460 miles), until they were stopped by the Johor Straits in the south – the end of the Asian mainland.

Sabah's and Sarawak's jungles were even more legendary, engulfing much of these states' total land area. The first great change in the landscape occurred scarcely a century ago when rubber trees grown from Amazonian seeds were so successful in experimental planting by the British that vast tracts of lowland Peninsular rainforests were cleared for plantations. This enterprise paved the way for future successful crops like oil palm, which outstripped rubber as the major agricultural crop in 1980, and which now engulfs the lowlands of every Malaysian state on both sides of the South China Sea. However, as these are tree crops, Malaysia's green and leafy character has been maintained, unlike other lands where the rainforests have been replaced by grassland.

Covering almost 132,000 square kilometres (51,000 square miles), Peninsular Malaysia contains 11 states, namely Johor, Kedah, Kelantan, Melaka (formerly Malacca), Negeri Sembilan, Pahang, Perak, Perlis, Pulau Pinang (Penang), Selangor, Terengganu, and the Federal Territory of Kuala Lumpur. Sarawak and Sabah in the north of Borneo, Malaysia's two largest states, occupy a total land area of around 200,000 square kilometres (78,000 square miles).

The entire length of the Peninsula's west coast is flanked by alluvial plains which often extend to 60 kilometres (37 miles) in width. These fertile flatlands are the reason that this coast has been the focus of settlements since the earliest days. Although the east coast also boasts a coastal plain, albeit slimmer than that of the west, the rugged interior was a formidable barrier against overland trade and as a result most of the trade routes were maritime.

Creating a magnificent jagged backdrop to the Peninsula, the granite mountains of the Banjaran Titiwangsa, also known as the Main Range, sprawl across the interior, reaching elevations from 900 to over 2,000 metres (2,950 to 6,600 feet) above sea level. The range extends from the Thai border in the north to Negeri Sembilan in the south, about three-quarters of the Peninsula's total length. Another sandstone range known as the Banjaran Timur engulfs much of the east coast states of Kelantan, Terengganu, and Pahang, and contains the Peninsula's highest peak, Gunung Tahan (2,191 metres; 7,188 feet) which crowns the vast, undisturbed tracts of the Taman Negara National Park.

Out of these rugged highlands are born the rivers, which not only nurture the land they flow through, but provided the only means of transport into the interior before the coming of roads and rail. They also engendered the establishment of many of today's political states. It is no coincidence that most of the peninsular states took their titles from the principal rivers flowing through them. Pahang is watered by the prodigious stream of the same name, the longest on the Malaysian mainland, which meanders for 475 kilometres (295 miles) from its source in the Cameron Highlands to empty into the South China Sea. However, statistics relating to both the mountains and the rivers of Malaysian Borneo, also known as East Malaysia, dwarf those of the Peninsula. The mountainous interior of Sabah is dominated by the jagged bulk of Mount Kinabalu which soars a spectacular 4,101 metres (13,455 feet) above the Crocker Range, its granite silhouette standing high above the treeline and often above the clouds. Not only is Kinabalu Malaysia's highest peak, but it is the loftiest summit between the Himalayas and New Guinea. This mountain's commanding role in the geography, lifestyle, and culture of Sabah is perhaps better understood when it is realized that Kinabalu is 1,450 metres (4,750 feet) higher than its nearest competitor, Gunung Trus Mardi – Malaysia's second-highest peak – also in the Crocker Range. Much of Sarawak's interior is also mountainous, particularly along its border with Indonesia, and its highest peaks, Gunung Murud (2,425 metres; 7,956 feet) and Gunung Mulu (2,371 metres; 7,779 feet), are also loftier than the highest mountains on the Peninsula.

At 563 kilometres (350 miles) in length, the Rajang River in Sarawak is Malaysia's longest waterway, navigable by steamers up to Kapit, 160 kilometres (100 miles) upstream. Sabah's Kinabatangan, which is only a little shorter, and the Baram (400 km or 250 miles) in northern Sarawak, also number among Borneo's great rivers. These deep, fast-flowing rivers are still widely used as important thoroughfares, offering a more direct means of transport to the inland centres of East Malaysia than the winding and often unpaved roads. It is infinitely more pleasant to sit back at ease in an air-conditioned express boat and observe the panorama of riverside life and longhouses along the verdant banks than to endure a dusty, bone-jangling bus ride through the new plantation towns. By comparison, only a few local ferry-boats still ply the Peninsular rivers which have long been bypassed by road and rail commuters. However, in the old days they too were vital arteries, particularly the old southern trading route which began in Johor at Muar, followed the river of the same name, and continued up the Semberong River, eventually reaching the east coast. Another ancient route which followed the Tembeling and Pahang Rivers from the east coast and through the Tasek Bera – a low-lying lake system – to the backlands of Melaka, was even used by an invading Thai army in the 15th century, who tried to conquer the kingdom of Melaka. Some geographers suspect that the Pahang River once flowed along this path to empty into the Melaka Straits before some geological change forced its rerouting to the east coast.

Mangrove forests fringe most of the west coast of the Peninsula and extensive areas of East Malaysia's coastline, particularly Sarawak and east of Sandakan in Sabah. Probably the most unlovely of all tropical habitats, with their tortuous root systems protruding above the gooey, grey mud-flats, coastal mangroves have only recently gained respect as an essential part of the environment.

Apart from a few beaches on the west coast, namely at Port Dickson, and on the islands of Penang and Pangkor, Malaysia's best beaches are the great strands of the Peninsula's east coast. Fringed by coconut palms and whispering casuarinas, their air misted from the salty trade winds of the South China Sea, the beaches extend from the Thai border in the far north of Kelantan to Johor in the south, only occasionally broken by river estuaries on which all the major east coast towns are situated.

Behind the beaches of the east coast are swamp forests containing stemless palms like the useful Nipa, which is woven for roofing material, and the thorny Pandanus which is used for baskets. Much of this type of countryside, especially on the Peninsula's west coast, has been drained by canals and reborn as oil palm and rubber plantations.

Thrusting from the green rice-fields of Perlis and Kedah, out of Perak's tin-rich Kinta Valley, and even as far south as Kuala Lumpur, are sheer-sided limestone massifs, their stark, white cliff-faces pitted with caves, and their summits cloaked in dwarf vegetation. Known in geological terms as 'tower karst', these limestone hills not only enliven the landscape, but have provided a home for humans since Stone Age times, evidenced by the archaeological remains that have been discovered in them. More recently, around a century ago the limestone massifs of Ipoh were discovered by Buddhist monks and the city is now renowned for its cathedral-like temple caves which draw thousands of pilgrims and visitors every year. Kuala Lumpur's Batu Caves are even more renowned, and the cave temple, sacred to Malaysia's Hindus, is the scene of a spectacular annual pilgrimage when 100,000 tranced penitents make the arduous climb to the clifftop shrine (see page 44). Again, however, East Malaysia outdoes the Peninsula, for not only are its cave systems longer, larger, and more spectacular, like Niah's Great Cave, but in the Gunung Mulu National Park, in northern Sarawak, the caverns are among the most superlative on the planet. The recently discovered Sarawak Chamber, a mind-boggling 16 football fields in size, is believed to be the world's largest cave chamber.

Malaysia's other diverse environments include the heath forests of Sarawak's Bako National Park, and the montane oak forests, the moss-covered 'cloud' forests, and the alpine scrub of the high country. Offshore, in the far north-west of the Peninsula, the Langkawi Islands are yet another geological marvel. Here, the steep-sided hills are made of marble, and before the islands' roads were recently upgraded to keep up with Langkawi's new jet-set resort status, they were still surfaced with crushed marble. Not so long ago it was the cheapest and most easily available material. Now, it is cut with high-powered saws and turned into bathrooms for the *nouveaux riches*.

The face of the land is forever changing. Most of the lowland forests have been cleared for plantations – some of them decades ago. Loggers have played havoc with tracts of the cathedral-like, once virgin rainforests. Highways cleave through the interior, opening up land that was once inaccessible to developers. Peat forests have been drained, lowering the coastal water table. Some residents claim that the climate is changing: that it is becoming hotter and dryer because the clearance of the forest has affected precipitation. But the scenario is not as bad as it sounds. International criticism of logging practices has succeeded in bringing about a downturn in the industry, but ironically the mills, especially on the Peninsula, were already finding quality logs difficult to come by. The realization that rainforests were under threat could not have come at a better time for Malaysia. The conservation movement continues to grow and as the people become better educated it is easier to make them more aware of the importance of protecting the environment for future generations. Moreover, Malaysia retains vast rainforests where the landscapes are still undisturbed, golden beaches where the only footsteps in the sand are yours, and tropical islands where it is still possible to emulate Robinson Crusoe.

## THE RAINFOREST

By all accounts F. Spenser Chapman was an experienced jungle basher. When the Japanese conquered the Malay Peninsula in 1942 he stayed behind, spending three and a half years with the guerrillas in the mountains, but even he was awed by the immensity of Malaysia's rainforests. He describes a 'nightmarish' journey across the Main Range in his book *The Jungle is Neutral*, published in 1949. He and a companion gained a summit by climbing across the tops of rhododendrons, which were so dense they actually supported their weight. 'From here,' Chapman wrote, 'there was one of the most wonderful views I have ever seen. For the first time I realised the terrifying vastness of the Malayan jungle.'

He was climbing in the ranges near Fraser's Hill, the hill station built by the British about two hours' drive north of Kuala Lumpur, and the vista of mauve-tinted hills swathed in trees, fading into the distance, is still magnificent. Sealed roads circle the resort and the rainforest grows

*The east coast railway under construction through the rainforests of Kelantan in 1922.*

right up to the back gardens of the bungalows and retreats. For the novice trekker there are a number of short trails that provide an introduction to the rainforest, and although they are tame stuff indeed compared to the undisturbed, virginal tracts deep in the mountains, the jungle is still thick enough to engulf the unwary if they wander off the track.

Before entering the rainforest to hunt or cut rattans, most Malays, even today, ask permission of the local spirits by uttering an invocation which explains that they come as friends, not enemies, that they are seeking a living, not making war, and they ask that the spirits will look after them until they return to their families. The aboriginal Orang Asli (literally 'original people') also believe that trouble will befall anyone who makes fun of the creatures of the forest. According to ancient Malay tales, which predate the coming of Islam and are still believed by many rural folk, the forests are peopled with spirits and ghosts. There are spectral hunters, the wailing of dead souls, disembodied heads which fly trailing their intestines, and even hauntingly beautiful perfumes that have the ability to lure men away from the trail. The Orang Asli believe in a host of *moyang*, demon ancestor spirits, who dwell in the midst of the forest. Charles Shuttleworth, who spent over two decades in Malaysian forests, wrote that he was with a group of aboriginals, and once with a Malay, when they saw forest spirits, but that he did not share their experience. Intriguingly, his feelings were that these creatures could have existed but that perhaps 'we westerners are too insensitive or out of harmony with our surroundings to see them'.

Once the rainforest is entered, most people have the idea that the going will be exceedingly rough, that the jungle-trekker must be forever hacking away with his machete in order to penetrate the dense undergrowth. This may well be true of *belukar*, regrowth forests which were formerly cleared, or along river-banks where the sunlight encourages rampant growth. In the depths of the true rainforest, however, where the lack of light creates a strange twilight effect even at midday, the forest floor is too dark to promote much growth, and is covered with leaf litter which is soft and springy underfoot, making walking comparatively easy.

Rays of sunlight filter through the forest canopy over 45 metres (150 feet) above the ground, but this scarcely lights up the gothic gloom. All about are the massive trunks of the Dipterocarps, the main tree family of the tropical rainforest, supported by muscular buttress roots. Like Grecian columns, their trunks rise smooth and branchless for at least two-thirds of their height. These are the timbers renowned for their resilience and durability. Among them is the reddish, sweet-smelling Chengal, the hardwood beloved by boat builders, and the lighter timbers like Meranti which are known by their Malay names the world over. Thrusting from the canopy, often attaining heights of up to 76 metres (250 feet), is the great Tualang, the tallest tree in the Malaysian rainforest. Viewed from a distance, its crown of greyish foliage is unmistakable, and from close up it is easy to see why the indigenous people believe that its gnarled crannies are the dwelling-places of spirits. Vines and creepers dangle from the canopy, draped about like the rigging on ancient sailing ships.

To the uninitiated, rainforest trees look extremely similar, but the Orang Asli of the Peninsula and the nomadic peoples of Borneo can identify every tree in their district, often hundreds of different species in a single hectare. In temperate forests, trees of the same species tend to occur together, but in the rainforest they grow in a more haphazard fashion and are scattered about, making identification even more confusing. Flowering and fruiting can also occur sporadically throughout the year, but the brilliant red hues of the new leaves can only be seen from above: 'For the eyes of God alone,' say the Malays.

In the sunny canopy the rainforest is alive with flowering orchids, and masses of ferns and epiphytes, like the notorious strangling fig which sends down its roots to the forest floor, encasing and probably eventually killing off its victim tree. Much of the colour of the rainforest is out of sight of trekkers on the ground, and the half-light even makes greens appear nearly black. Often a delicate bloom lying on the trail, or a lingering perfume, is the only indication that high above a tree is in full blossom. But then, a glossy, red spike of a flowering ginger is spied, lighting up the gloom, or a butterfly with ultramarine wings flashes past, or the lucky trekker may be rewarded with a glimpse of the scarlet-hued *Rafflesia*, the world's largest flower. This rare monster, which can grow nearly a metre (three feet) wide is actually a parasite which lives off a liana. It is usually smelt before it is seen, however, as its nauseating stench is as legendary as its size.

Conservationists stress the importance of preserving the rainforest because of its incredible abundance of medicinal plants, few of which are known to science. However, the indigenous peoples have known since time immemorial about the healing properties of the trees and plants which grow in their regions. Failing to find a cure in hospital for his allergic reaction to the poisonous Rengas tree, an experienced botanist took the advice of local people and cured it with a foul-smelling vine translated as 'the farting leaf'.

After the cathedral-like atmosphere of the rainforest, with its dappled light and absence of sunshine, the equatorial brightness of the cleared lands outside the forest comes as a shock to those who have become accustomed to life inside. Sarawak's pale-skinned Penan, the hunter-gatherers of the forest, feared broad daylight and rarely ventured outside the deep shade of the trees. Their 'high standard of physical development and vigour', which was noted by Charles Hose early this century, contrasts rather markedly with the general health of the present-day Penan who have chosen to live in resettlement camps in the cleared land. It is little wonder that some Penan still opt for their original nomadic existence deep in the rainforest, as for them it is home. After 15 months of living and working on the 1977-8 Royal Geographical Society expedition into Gunung Mulu National Park in Sarawak, the explorer Robin Hanbury-Tenison still felt that the rainforest was a mysterious place that would never be fully understood. For all their recording and analysing in the world's richest environment, he realized that the scientific knowledge needed to probe these forests adequately was 'beyond the capacity of one man, one group or even one nation.'

*Georgetown, Penang, 1811: an engraving by James Wathen showing the cluster of red-roofed houses that still characterizes the old town. A British East India Company naval base had been set up here in 1786 and when the island was declared a duty-free port traders, particularly the Chinese, flocked in. Penang flourished, although the founding of the even more successful port of Singapore in 1819 diminished its importance. One result of this has been that the original buildings remain comparatively well preserved.*

## THE COAST

A Chinese sailor's song of the 17th century tells of 'being escorted by favourable winds' to Pahang where he trades his wares for turtle shells. 'One fine comb I will save for my wife. The others I will sell . . .'

The Chinese had been sailing into the warm shallow waters of the South China Sea for at least a millennium before this verse was penned, lured not only by the quality of the tortoiseshell, but also for the black coral, the *trepang* (a sea slug coveted by Chinese gourmets), cowrie shells that were used as an early form of currency, and the glutinous edible birds' nests – a prized delicacy – gathered from the ceilings of caves on offshore islands. Ancient traders put in at the coastal ports to barter their goods for those of the interior; silks were exchanged for rhinoceros horn, porcelain for camphor. Mariners, guided by the unmistakable twin granite peaks of Pulau Tioman, found safe anchorage in sheltered coves even during the fierce north-east monsoon. In the towering rainforests of the interior, which even today still start just behind the beaches, early seamen found timbers to mend their boats, fibres for making ropes, aromatic woods to augment their cargoes, game and fruits for their larders, and crystal-clear freshwater streams.

Today, if you sail up the Peninsula's east coast, much of the coastline still looks as it did in those days. Beaches stretch to either horizon, and the estuary ports remain dependent on the tide and the seasons. Even the tourist ferries which ply from Mersing to Pulau Tioman and the dozens of other offshore islands run according to the tides, and the sand-bars at the river-mouth are just as tricky to manoeuvre through as they ever were. The greatest change to the east coast scenery occurs on the Terengganu coast, where oil-rigs cluster offshore and, on the shoreline, fishing villages have given way to a huge petroleum and natural gas complex.

Although oil and gas extraction has boosted the state's revenues, most of the coastal families depend on the sea for a living. Fresh fish is an essential everyday part of the diet of the east coast Malays even when they can afford chicken or other meat, a fact that surprised Munshi Abdullah, the scribe to Thomas Stamford Raffles, founder of Singapore, when he journeyed to the east coast in the early 19th century. When fresh fish are not available, salted fish is the preferred alternative. All along the coast villagers salt and dry fish, but at Beserah, just north of Kuantan, drying-racks made of split bamboo line the entire front of the fishing village. Just after dawn the sarong-clad workers lay the salted fish out on the racks, then during the morning they are turned to ensure that they are correctly dried. Around mid-afternoon the fishing boats return from the offshore grounds and the village comes to life. A couple of drowsy water buffaloes are hitched to a cart, a turbaned villager goads them into action, and they thunder down the beach and into the surf. Here, the fish are transferred into rattan baskets on the cart while the buffaloes wait patiently, thigh-deep in the waves. Elsewhere, this scene is a rarity these days, as Beserah is probably the only Malaysian community that continues to use this method of transporting the day's catch to the shore.

Offshore, often protected by islands, and resembling a wooden hut perched on precariously thin legs, are traditional Malay fishing traps known as *kelong*. Wooden stakes driven into the sea-bed like an aquatic fence channel the fish towards the trap, and at night the light streaming from the generator attracts the tiny anchovies, or *ikan bilis*, into the huge net which hangs just below the surface. When it is full it is winched up on to the platform, where the anchovies are scooped out of the net and transferred into wicker baskets which are lowered into vats of boiling sea-water and cooked on the spot. After drying, this mainstay of Malay cuisine is then used for *sambal*, a hot spicy sauce eaten with rice, fried with peanuts for a tasty snack, or pounded and used as a flavouring in a variety of savoury dishes.

Called 'the Ladies Sea' by the Portuguese because of their apparently placid nature, the Melaka Straits are often so calm that scarcely a ripple disturbs their mirror-like surface. The sea and the sky often seem to merge together with no perceptible horizon, and boats hover offshore, the tropical glare creating an illusion that they are actually floating above the surface. Sometimes, though, the Straits show their fickle character, especially during the south-west monsoon. Then, afternoon storms known as Sumatras, from their nearby place of origin, throw the waters into a frenzy, sinking ships and battering the coast with unusually high waves.

Flanking the Melaka Straits from the Thai border in the north to the Straits of Johor in the south, the coast is virtually an unbroken expanse of mangrove forests, which extend from one to 12 kilometres (1000 yards to 7 miles) across. The labyrinthine passages between the dense mangrove stands offered a safe haven to the pirate bands which have plundered the shipping lane since earliest times. Piracy is still a problem. These days they use speed-boats and throw grappling hooks up over the decks of oil-freighters. However, most of the present buccaneers originate from the Indonesian side, and Malaysia is spearheading the effort to rid the Straits of pirates once and for all.

'To try and walk in it is to risk broken ankles,' wrote the naturalist Charles Shuttleworth, describing the tortuous root system of the mangrove which protrudes above the mud-flats in order to obtain oxygen. These fast-growing trees – some species can grow a centimetre in an hour – help to expand the coastline by trapping river silt in their roots which eventually becomes natural reclaimed land. The trees' method of propagation is as bizarre as their shape. Seeds germinate attached to the branch, then a long root grows downwards ensuring that when the seed falls into the mud it will be able to take root instantly.

A wide variety of palms grow in the lowland swampy regions behind the mangrove forests. There is the versatile Nipa, a trunkless palm used for making roof-thatching known as *atap*, and the Nibong with its slender but resilient trunk used as foundation-posts for fishing platforms, or formerly split and used for flooring. The graceful Areca palm provides the betel-nut which when chewed with *sireh*, the leaf of the betel vine, and a dab of lime, stimulates the user into a mild sense of well-being. This practice is now only popular with the elderly, but it was once rampant throughout South-east Asia. The chewer's teeth are stained a bright red from the juice, and the Victorian traveller Isabella Bird remarked that in her day, 'The Malays think that you look like a beast if you have white teeth!'

Coastal Malaysia always was, and still is, the preferred habitation of the Malays in both Peninsular and East Malaysia. Their original lifestyle was supported by this environment. The seas gave them fish and seafood, the mangrove swamps provided shellfish, and essentials for house-building, the coconut palms they planted along the foreshore provided milk, oil, fibres, brooms, and had a host of other uses. Evidence of the Malays' intimate relationship with the sea is found all over Malaysia but nowhere so strongly as on the Peninsular east coast. The palm-fringed coast is still lined with picturesque fishing villages where wooden houses on stilts shelter from the monsoon's wrath behind palm-thatched fences. Here, the beach is the backyard, and villagers still plan their lives around the rhythm of the sea, the daily catch, the annual monsoon and the lunar cycles.

## THE MOUNTAINS

Since earliest times Malaysia's mountains have been shrouded in mystery. Gunung Ledang, known as Mount Ophir to the British, a lone peak behind Melaka, was the home of a legendary princess whose beauty was so incomparable that a 15th-century sultan tried all manner of ruses to woo her. But he was eventually defeated by her dowry list. The seven trays of mosquitoes' hearts did not deter him but the cup of his son's blood was deemed too great a price.

Sabah's Mount Kinabalu, named from the Kadazan for 'The Revered Abode of the Dead', was believed to be such hallowed soil that early explorers had to sacrifice a white cockerel and make an offering of seven eggs to appease the spirits at Panar Laban, the site of the present overnight huts, which means 'the place of sacrifice'. Until half a century ago, however, a more sinister ritual was conducted, for it was not unusual for the Kadazan to kill a prisoner in order that he might take a message to a departed relative whose soul resided on the mountain. He was tied to a tree, or imprisoned in a bamboo cage, while his captors danced around him and prodded him to death with spears. Each prod was accompanied by a message to be sent to their deceased kin.

Gunung Chini, a jagged mountain behind Tasek Chini, a lake system in Pahang's interior, is believed by the local Orang Asli to be the home of a *naga*, a dragon-like water serpent which is said to inhabit and guard the depths of the lake. Many of these formerly mystical peaks have now been well and truly climbed and explored. However, as few climbers wander far from the main trail, and as the montane forests are notoriously dense, unlike the lowland rainforests, there are still many inaccessible areas that retain their mystery. Even Gunung Ledang, which is crowded with climbers every weekend, is still accorded its legendary status: local *bomoh* (traditional medicine-men cum magicians) still reputedly acquire their esoteric knowledge from the immortal princess who resides in a cave on the peak.

Although by Himalayan standards Malaysian mountains are not all that high (with the exception of Mount Kinabalu), they are notoriously difficult to climb. Gunung Tahan, the Peninsula's highest peak, stands only 2,187 metres (7,175 feet) above sea-level, but its remote location turns the climb into a nine-day expedition. The heat, humidity, the ubiquitous leeches, and the arduous treks – the second day's route traverses 26 hills – take their toll on bodies not accustomed to trekking in the tropics. But for those who can endure the discomforts the rewards more than make up for the effort required.

On the Gunung Tahan climb it takes four days to reach the montane oak forests at 1,100 metres (3,600 feet), but on Kinabalu this type of forest surrounds the chalets at park headquarters and embraces half of the national park's 754 square kilometres (290 square miles). Tropical trees are much less evident at this altitude, and the oaks, chestnuts, laurels, and myrtles that abound are representative of families found in temperate regions. However, the resemblance to such climes ends here as these montane forests are bedecked with a abundance of epiphytes, orchids and mosses, and even the acorns are the size of oranges. Because the trees are smaller, and their canopies not as wide or dense, more sunlight filters through to the forest floor making for denser undergrowth than is found in the lowland forests.

At around 1,800 metres (5,900 feet), the exquisite 'cloud forests' begin. Perpetually wreathed in cloud, these forests of gnarled conifers and rhododendrons are swathed in mosses, orchids, and lichens and embellished with delicate bamboos and thorny rattans. During the flowering seasons the pinks, apricots, reds, purples and whites of the showy rhododendrons enliven the scenery, while pitcher plants – carnivorous oddities of the plant world – dangle beside the trail to trap unwary insects. The pitchers of *Nepenthes raja*, the largest of all the species, were used as water-carriers by the native porters in Spencer St John's early expeditions up Mount Kinabalu, and he noted that one particularly large specimen held about two litres (four pints). An even more famous expeditionist, Edward Shackleton, tells of the dense moss forests he encountered on his 1932 ascent of Sarawak's Gunung Mulu, which was until his ascent widely regarded as unclimbable. It was impossible for the party to tell whether they were walking on land or over the tops of trees, for the 'mountain-side seemed almost to disappear under the all-enveloping moss forest'. However, his view of the summit peak protruding through a crown of scarlet rhododendrons in full blossom must have more than made up for the rigours of the climb. After his porters had spent a freezing night at the presumed summit shivering in their loin-cloths, the clouds parted at dawn to reveal another even higher peak nearby. Shackleton pressed on and called the highest point Oxford Peak, in honour of the university which sponsored his expedition. Fortunately, although he maintained that the name-change had been approved by the Rajah, Charles Vyner Brooke, common sense prevailed, and the mountain, together with the national park that surrounds it, is still known by its original name of Gunung Mulu.

Above the bonsai tea-trees and the dwarf rhododendrons, the treeline is reached at Mount Kinabalu's highest overnight camp, Sayat Sayat (3,800 metres; 12,500 feet). From here, the great, granite summit soars unimpeded into a star-filled, cobalt-blue sky. Striated by glaciers from the last Ice Age, the rock-cap of the summit becomes a huge waterfall during the rainy season. Geologists say the mountain is still growing – at around five millimetres (a quarter of an inch) a year – and equipped with this knowledge climbers often feel as if they are scaling the backbone of some huge primeval creature. 'The Revered Abode of the Dead' seems an apt title for such an awesome peak on the roof of Malaysia.

## THE WILDLIFE

### Mammals

Malaysia's fauna, although impressive in its sheer number of species, is notoriously difficult to see. Peninsular Malaysia is home to more than 200 of South-east Asia's estimated 300 species of mammals. Travellers who have viewed the great herds of the African savannah, however, may well leave Malaysia with the impression that there is no wildlife there, a remark which is often overheard at Taman Negara, the nation's oldest national park. The animals certainly are there, but they are masters of survival and camouflage and in the rainforest they can remain invisible to the uninitiated even at close quarters.

The largest of all Malaysian mammals, the Asian Elephant, which is somewhat smaller than the African species, has ears that measure one and a half metres (five feet) across, and a correspondingly acute sense of hearing. These massive herbivores spend their nights devouring bamboo thickets, groves of wild bananas, and sometimes a newly planted plantation (which usually leads to its undoing) in order to consume their daily diet of around 300 kilograms (660 pounds) of fodder each. As dawn approaches they retreat into the dense rainforest far from human haunts to rest during the hot daylight hours. During the colonial days before elephant hunting was outlawed, these great ungulates, known to the Malays as *gajah*, were considered a prestigious trophy. Instructions on how to hunt them showed what a superb sense of smell they possess. It was advisable always to be to windward of the beast, though this was well-nigh impossible most of the time, as the wind eddies constantly change direction in the forest. One handbook suggests 'striking matches every minute or so while approaching an elephant', and even this method did not guarantee success, as the elephant was quite likely, even with the greatest precautions, to 'get one's wind and vanish'. The big-game hunters of the colonial era were interested in hunting elephants only for trophies like the ghastly Victorian umbrella stands made from elephant's feet, but in the early days the Malays hunted them in order to catch and tame them. Travel by elephant-back was *de*

*Elephants in ceremonial regalia crossing a river around 1920.*

*rigueur* for royalty and the upper class until the early 1900s, and photographs from the period even show tin-prospectors and British administrators travelling in this mode. Sultans kept herds of specially bred elephants for ceremonial occasions, a practice that was already well established in the 15th-century Melakan sultanate. In the *Sejarah Melayu*, the court annals of this time, Sultan 'Abdu'l-Jamal of Pahang urges a royal visitor to 'Tarry awhile and let us noose elephants, for at this season elephants will be coming down from the hills and noosing elephants is rare sport!' These magnificent giants of the rainforest once roamed from one end of the Peninsula to the other, but today their original habitats have been greatly reduced by rampant clearing for plantations. They still exist in moderate numbers in the interior rainforests, especially in the more remote parts of Taman Negara and in the Perak forests along the East-West Highway, where some elephants from endangered habitats have been relocated by wildlife authorities.

In East Malaysia, elephants are found only on Sabah's east coast. According to a popular tale they are the descendants of a small herd which was given to the Sultan of Sulu by the East India Company in 1750. However, Ferdinand Magellan's chronicler, Antonio Pigafetta, had written of Bornean elephants two centuries before this, and a bone from an elephant's foot found in Sarawak's Niah Caves proves that ungulates had roamed Borneo since Neolithic times.

Another large, but lesser known Malaysian herbivore is the *seladang* or Gaur, the largest wild ox in the world which can weigh up to 1,500 kilograms (one and a half tons). Standing almost two metres (seven feet) at the shoulder, these powerful beasts with their huge curved horns were by far the most difficult quarry for the big-game hunter as their ferocity when aroused and their ability to recover when wounded were legendary. They are occasionally glimpsed from hides in Taman Negara and left undisturbed in their native habitat they are normally unaggressive.

With its strange markings – black front and legs and white body – and its trunk-like proboscis, the pony-sized Tapir, found only in Peninsular Malaysia, is probably the strangest and most gentle of the herbivores. Although its colouring would appear to stand out in the forest, it actually helps to camouflage the Tapir when it is feeding on moonlit nights.

In imminent danger of extinction through hunting, because their horns are prized by Chinese herbalists for their fever-reducing properties, the Sumatran (or Asian Two-horned) Rhinoceros now numbers only around 15 individuals in Sabah. In the Endau-Rompin region of the Peninsula there is a population of around 20 individuals – the world's largest – and sightings have occasionally been made in Taman Negara.

Undisputed king of the jungle, and still found in reasonable numbers, the Tiger is Malaysia's national animal: two snarling specimens support the country's coat of arms with their paws. No other creature inspires such respect, or is the subject of as much folklore, as the Malayan Tiger. Its striped markings make it extremely difficult to spot in the rainforest, where the shadow-play can render a Tiger invisible even at close quarters. Because of this, and their ability to sense a person long before he knows of their existence, they are seldom seen. Most indigenous people are quite happy with this situation, for although attacks on humans are rare, the tiger commands an almost supernatural place in Malay mythology. The Portuguese chronicler, Godinho de Eredia, tells of the wild Banua people who terrorized the inhabitants of Melaka with their ability to change into tigers. They had apparently learnt their black arts from the Princess of Gunung Ledang (a mountain behind Melaka), where, legend has it, even today, *bomoh* acquire their magic skills. Although Tigers will attack people only when provoked, when injured or extremely infirm, or when protecting their young, anyone who has glimpsed a fresh footprint (dinner-plate sized), or heard their roar in the dense rainforest, can well understand the reaction of an Orang Asli guide in Endau-Rompin who said that after seeing a tiger you can't eat for a week.

Leopards and a variety of smaller native cats also roam the rainforest, but like their more famous kin, the Tiger, they are seldom seen. Clouded Leopards, with their python-like markings, are particularly attractive. A bird-watcher in Negeri Sembilan recently caught a glimpse of one reclining on a tree-branch quite close to the road. It was so beautifully camouflaged, however, that he only noticed it by accident when training his binoculars on a nearby bird. Clouded Leopards and other cats are found in Malaysian Borneo, but Tigers occur only on the mainland, although evidence from archaeological digs in Sarawak's Niah Caves suggests that they could have existed there in the Stone Age.

Seldom attaining more than one and a half metres (five feet) in height, Malaysia's principal omnivore, the Honey Bear, or Sun Bear, has a reputation which far outweighs its size. With its irritable and unpredictable temper, even tigers go out of their way to avoid the *beruang*. After it has satiated itself on bees' nests or ant larvae, the Honey Bear makes a peculiar noise which has been described as sounding like the purr of an electric refrigerator.

Monkeys are Malaysia's most easily seen mammals. Long-tailed Macaques are known to the Malays as *kera*, from the sound they make (most Malay animal names are onomatopoeic). They are commonly seen harassing picnickers all along the coast from Port Dickson to Penang. Larger, Pig-tailed Macaques, called *beruk*, can often be seen on the east coast, and in Kedah and Perlis, riding pillion on motorcycles with their trainers as they travel about between *kampungs* collecting coconuts. While young, they are trained to climb the palms, select the ripe drinking coconuts and screw them off with their feet. In his prime, a *beruk* has been known to gather a staggering 700 coconuts in one day.

Usually heard before they are seen, the attractive, grey and white Leaf Monkeys, known as *lotong*, are often glimpsed crashing from one branch to another. In the oil-palm plantations, they clamber along a frond until it bends with their weight and then leap for another, the whole tribe noisily in tow as if playing 'follow the leader'. In comparison, the gibbons – the fastest wingless travellers of the forest – swing silently through their arboreal abode like adepts of the high trapeze. The ebony-coloured *siamang* lives in the higher montane forests and has a goitre-like protuberance under its jaw that helps to produce the marvellous whooping calls that echo through the forests. The White-handed and Dark-handed Gibbons, collectively named *wak-wak* by the Malays for their characteristic sound, live in the lower realms and are more easily sighted than the reclusive *siamang*.

The gibbons' song is well known to anyone who has spent time in the Malaysian forest. After he retired to France, Henri Fauconnier, the prize-winning writer of *The Soul of Malaya*, and an ex-plantation manager, often talked of his nostalgia for jungle sounds, so in 1970 his former Malayan colleagues sent him a recording of rainforest noises including the calls of the *wak-wak* and *siamang*. Three years later when he died, his daughter discovered that the last recording he had listened to was this one of the sounds which he missed most during his retirement.

Its name literally meaning 'man of the forest', the intelligent and charming Orang-utan is the most famous of all Malaysian primates, and is remarkably humanoid in its behaviour. These orange-coloured apes live only in the forests of Borneo and Sumatra, and have suffered near-genocide since the last century. When Alfred Russel Wallace, naturalist and colleague of Darwin, studied Orang-utans in the 1850s, they numbered in tens of thousands, but today they are an endangered species. At Sabah's Sepilok Forest Reserve, orphaned and previously captive Orang-utans are rehabilitated into the wild. Since its foundation as a sanctuary in 1964, over 200 animals have been successfully re-educated and some have now mated with wild apes. Naturally playful, Orang-utans never fail to delight a crowd, which is partly why they have been so exploited by zoos. Park brochures at Sepilok advise visitors to keep an eye on their belongings, but recently a French visitor found to his embarrassment that it was not only his hat that caught an Orang-utan's attention, as he was systematically stripped of all his clothing. Was it the wily ape's way of turning the tables on us?

Known to the Malays as *orang belanda*, which means 'Dutchman', the Proboscis Monkey, which occurs only in Borneo, is characterized by its large pendulous nose. However, this appendage is only outsized on the male of the species, which is also much larger in body weight than the female. Their superb colouring ranges from maroon to a yellowish brown on the upper back, with a greyish or yellow tone on the lower back, belly and tail.

Malaysia is inhabited by five kinds of deer: the *rusa* or Sambar Deer, the *kijang* or Barking Deer (of which there are two species), and the Greater and Lesser Mouse-deer. The Lesser Mouse-deer, known as either *pelandok* or *kancil*, is by far the best-known, as it is the hero of many Malay folk stories where it outwits larger creatures like tigers and elephants in the style of Brer Rabbit. This minuscule creature, which is a closer relative of the camel than the deer, has tiny hoofs about the size of a pencil and stands a mere 20 centimetres (eight inches) at the shoulder. Relentlessly hunted because of its sweet, tender flesh, the Lesser Mouse-deer is now a protected animal but this does not deter some determined gourmands. Recently, wildlife authorities discovered that mouse-deer was still featured on the menu of a Pulau Tioman restaurant enthusiastically frequented by Singaporeans.

Of the 200 species of mammal in Peninsular Malaysia, two-thirds are either fruit-eating or insect-eating bats. They are an indispensable part of the rainforest ecosystem. At dawn on Pulau Tioman, colonies of Flying Foxes noisily compete for hanger space in the coconut palms, and every evening in Sarawak's Gunung Mulu National Park, great clouds of bats make their exit from the cavernous Deer Cave for their nightly forage in the forest.

Other Malaysian mammals include the Wild Dog, or *serigala*, a rare creature which looks similar to an English fox; several species of civets, which resemble a large, shaggy mongoose; mongooses proper which live off snakes and small mammals; otters, squirrels, flying squirrels, and the bizarre Pangolin, or Scaly Anteater, which rolls itself into an armoured ball in self-defence.

### Birds

Every year thousands of bird-watchers gather at Fraser's Hill, a resort 1,500 metres (5,000 feet) up in the range to the north-east of Kuala Lumpur, for the International Bird Race. Bird-life is prolific here in the montane forest, as it is within the ranges of both lowland and mountain species and is also on a major migration route. Many of the Peninsula's 620 bird species can be glimpsed without even having to penetrate the jungle, as the lush forest grows right up to the edge of the sealed roads. Eagles silently drift by, almost out of sight, high up in the thermal currents, while a cackling in the treetops and a whooshing of wings reveals a hornbill with its strange head casque and huge curved bill. Perhaps the most amazing sight of all is when the formerly quiet rainforest suddenly breaks into birdsong as a 'bird wave' appears, in which dozens of different species such as orioles, babblers, and nuthatches fly together as a mixed flock.

Malaysia's most distinctive birds are the hornbills, with their black and white plumage, and their distinctively shaped casques and bills which give rise to the names of the various species. The Rhinoceros Hornbill has a red casque shaped like the horn of its namesake; the Helmeted Hornbill looks as if it is wearing an ancient Roman helmet. Their nesting habits are just as intriguing. When nesting begins the female climbs into a tree-hole. The male then plasters her in with mud, effectively imprisoning her, not only for the incubation of the eggs but also during the early days of rearing the chicks. During her long internment, though, she is not neglected, as the devoted male feeds her berries and fruit through a small opening.

Over half of Malaysia's bird species are found in the rainforest, and around 70 live exclusively in the montane regions from 1,000 to 1,500 metres (3,300 to 5,000 feet) above sea-level. Each species inhabits a certain level of the rainforest. Pheasants, peafowls, jungle fowls, quails, and pittas stay on the jungle floor; broadbills and trogons reside in the mid-storey; minivets, flower-peckers and leafbirds flitter about the canopy.

One of Malaysia's most brilliantly feathered birds, which was always difficult to glimpse but is seldom seen these days, is the rare Argus Pheasant, better known by its Malay name *kuang* which describes its distinctive, piercing call. Four of the most colourful of the pheasants are now on the verge of extinction.

Even more colourful than the rare pheasants, but much smaller in size, are the jewel-hued flower-peckers, sunbirds, and spiderhunters of the rainforest. The Crimson

Sunbird's brilliant red head and back is off-set by a metallic purple tail, a yellow lower back and a grey belly, while the Scarlet-backed Flower-pecker and the Orange-bellied Flower-pecker are as colourful as their names suggest.

Keeping songbirds is a popular hobby throughout Malaysia and certain species are prized for their calls. Doves, commonly known by their Malay name *tekukur*, make the sound of their name in the early morning. To the enthusiast, the different stress that the bird puts on each syllable, the tone of the voice and other qualities all combine to produce a sound which varies from one bird to the other. To the uninitiated at a bird-singing contest, however, the dozens of doves in their bamboo cages set high on poles (they sing better at this height), sound monotonously the same. But if the call of the *tekukur* is not to everyone's liking, the song of the Common Shama is music to the ears. A type of thrush, known by its Malay name of *murai hutan*, this silver-voiced bird is the most highly prized of all the Malaysian songbirds.

Probably the world's best talking bird, with its uncanny ability to mimic other birds, is the *burung tiong*, a species of grackle. This large mynah is often trapped in the forest when young and then taught to talk. Another excellent mimic, and a favourite bird to watch flying through the rainforest, is the Large Racquet-tailed Drongo. Its metallic black plumage flashes past, lighting up the gloom, with its strange tail dangling behind it like a feathery pendant.

The members of the kingfisher family are also brilliantly coloured and easy to spot. There are 13 different species, but the White-breasted Kingfisher, with its colourful turquoise wings and back, sitting on poles, electric wires, or bushes waiting to dive into roadside canals, is the species that every traveller to Malaysia will have seen at least once. Of the 27 different species of bulbul with their characteristic crests, some live in forests but many are often seen along rivers and in gardens and cultivated areas.

Mangrove forests and their surrounding mud-flats attract many different species of migratory shorebirds like plovers, curlews, snipes, herons, egrets, and storks. The largest of these is the Lesser Adjutant Stork, an incredibly ugly bird with a hairless head and knobbly legs.

Malay nomenclature frequently describes birds with uncanny accuracy. Often, the name does not reflect the bird's appearance, as many Western names do, but either the sound of its song, or an association with its song, such as the *burung tukang*, literally 'workman bird', which describes the barbet's 'tonk-tonk' voice sounding like a tinsmith at work. For the novice bird-watcher the Malay name is a great help in identifying bird calls. An example is a type of cuckoo, evocatively called the Brain-Fever Bird: the Malays call it *burung anak mati*, 'bird whose child is dead', because its call is reminiscent of the melancholic cry of a mourning mother. Owls are perfectly described as *burung hantu*, 'ghost birds', because of their eerie sounds and silent flight. Malaysian bird names could easily constitute a volume on their own, for every name has a story to tell, like that of the colourful Hooded Pitta. Called *gembala pelandok*, or 'mouse-deer herdsman' in Malay, this title conjures up a marvellous image of these delightful birds running around the forest floor rounding up the equally diminutive mouse-deer.

### Fish

Some fish climb trees, others shoot their prey by squirting water, and another has been known to lure monkeys out of trees – such are the acclaimed oddities of Malaysian rivers. The first of these is the so-called Climbing Perch, which is not really a perch but a gourami. Its additional breathing gills enable it to travel across the land. Experts say it does not really climb trees, but the name was given to it by a 19th-century traveller who claimed to have spied one up a tree. The capabilities of the Archer Fish, however, are not disputed by naturalists. True to its name, this amazing marksman takes aim at an insect which is either flying above the water or on an overhanging branch; by squirting pressurized water through its mouth the fish hits the insect and knocks it into the water.

Malaysia's biggest freshwater fish, the aptly named Giant Catfish, or *ikan tapah*, can grow to almost a metre (three feet) long and weigh around 45 kilograms (100 pounds). As befitting such a monster, the legends attributed to it are equally remarkable. Dogs and even mouse-deer have been attacked and eaten while swimming in rivers, and according to a Malay saying they even have the power to mesmerize monkeys with their stare: the tranced simian falls helpless into the water and is devoured.

Another most unusual fish is the pop-eyed mudskipper, a familiar and comical sight in the mangrove forests. Like the Climbing Perch, it is equipped to breathe out of water, and it waddles around the mud-flats at low tide, supported by its pectoral fins which act as legs.

Many freshwater fish are excellent eating and provide good sport for anglers. Those in the know head to the fishing lodges in the backwaters of Taman Negara, the National Park, to fish for Sebarau, a good eating carp; Kelah, also known as the 'Malayan Mahseer'; the Toman or 'Snake-head'; and the best fighting fish of all, the leaping Kelesa.

Malaysia's waters are also the home of many well-known aquarium fish like the silvery and orange-hued Harlequin, and the smallest of all Malaysian fish, the red-and-black-spotted *Rasbora maculata*, which is only two and a half centimetres (one inch) in length. Known for their belligerence towards other males, their vigilance in guarding the nest (the female often eats the eggs), and prized by collectors for their graceful appearance, Siamese Fighting Fish are commonly found in freshwater ponds.

Saltwater fish comprise dozens of different varieties and form the basis of the Malaysian diet. There is the diamond-shaped Pomfret, a favourite steaming fish of the Chinese, said to be more delicious than the turbot; *ikan tenggiri*, the Spanish Mackerel which is best grilled over charcoal; *ikan tongkol*, a tunny popular on the east coast; and the incomparable Grouper, to name a few.

### Reptiles and Amphibians

Although Malaysia is home to over 100 species of snakes they are not often sighted by visitors, as the dense vegetation provides a perfect camouflage. Probably the best-known and most often viewed of all the species is Wagler's Pit Viper. These are found by the dozen draped about the altars and furniture at Penang's Snake Temple. Soon after the temple was founded in 1850 these poisonous vipers arrived and they have made their home here ever since. Worshippers believe that they are holy representations of the temple deity, Choor Soo Kong. They sleep in the temple during the day – some say their somnolent state is caused by the incense smoke – then at night they feed on eggs donated by the devotees. Vipers which have had their poison removed are daubed with red spots on their heads: these may be draped around visitors' necks for bizarre photography sessions.

The most deadly and feared of all the species is the King Cobra, said by some to be completely unafraid of humans, which can attain over five metres (16 feet) in length. However, it is only really dangerous when guarding its nest, on which the female sits while the male stalks the perimeter. Another cobra, known as *ular sendok*, the 'spoon-shaped snake', because of its characteristic cobra hood, can spit venom into its victim's eyes. If the poison is not immediately washed out it can permanently damage one's sight, and even if it is cleansed the affected area is still painful for days.

Three species of krait, which are also very poisonous, live in Malaysia, but they seldom bite people and are very unaggressive. Their colouring is nothing short of spectacular. The Banded Krait is striped in yellow and black, the Malaysian Krait has alternate bands of white and black, and the Red-head Krait has a metallic blue back, red head, neck and tail, and a white belly. Coral snakes are also extremely colourful and their venom is very toxic but they rarely attack humans.

South American boa-constrictors and anacondas have always been described as the largest snakes on the planet. However, the world's largest snake is actually the Reticulated Python, which resides in Malaysia. Growing up to nine metres (30 feet) in length, and weighing up to 127 kilograms (280 pounds), these beautiful creatures with giraffe-like markings are often seen lying across the full width of plantation roads. They are extremely slow-moving if they have just dined – after a good meal they can sleep for a week – and are easily captured when in this state. Non-venomous tree-snakes are amongst the most beautifully coloured of all Malaysian species. The Paradise Tree-snake is black with red spots and a greenish-yellow belly, and is credited with being able to 'fly', a feat it accomplishes by moving fast along a branch and then gliding through the air with its body flattened. Tales of this feat would be enough to deter many would-be explorers, except that these snakes usually only use this skill to cross rivers and are not in the habit of accosting passers-by.

Around 80 species of lizards are found in Malaysia. By far the most common is the Common House Gecko, better known by its Malay name *cik cak* (pronounced 'chick chack'), which describes the sound it makes. These translucent little creatures scuttle across ceilings stalking insects, then watch in frozen immobility before pouncing, a practice which gives rise to the old Malay saying that the gecko always pauses before the kill to give his victim time to say his prayers.

The largest of all the lizard species is the Water Monitor Lizard, known in Malay as *biawak*. Attaining a size of around two and a half metres (eight feet) in length, this great lizard is often sighted lumbering around plantations and swimming in lakes and rivers. They often come right up to the backs of Malay *kampungs* and as they are scavengers they can usually be seen picking through the kitchen waste, especially after a village feast.

Crocodiles once inhabited all of Malaysia's rivers, but after being relentlessly hunted for their skins they are now quite scarce on the Peninsula, although very recently they have made a comeback on the banks of the Melaka River and have even been sighted in the vicinity of the town. The author has also observed crocodiles sunning themselves on the banks of the Sedili River in south-eastern Johor. Estuarine Crocodiles, also known as Saltwater Crocodiles, are Malaysia's most common species. In Sarawak where they grow to an enormous size, a few man-killers have been encountered even in recent years. The formidable reputation of these saurians is no doubt attributable to the legends that surround them. In Johor, a famous *bomoh* still lives on Sungai Buaya, 'The Crocodile River', lending credence to the old tale that magicians exercised control over crocodiles.

Eleven different water tortoises and three species of land tortoises make their home in Malaysia. The most common and easily spotted is a species of terrapin which has an unusual turned-up nose, leading some observers to mistake it for a snake in the water. Tortoises can be seen in their hundreds at the government breeding centre at Bota Kanan on the Perak River.

At Rantau Abang, a long, sandy beach in Terengganu, giant Leatherback Turtles come ashore every year to lay their eggs. Weighing over 350 kilograms (770 pounds) and measuring up to one and a half metres (five feet) in length, these are the world's largest marine turtles, and this stretch of sand is one of their last remaining nesting-sites in the world. In former years, eggs were collected indiscriminately, and turtle-watching was a carnival-like event, but these days tourists are strictly controlled and the taking of eggs is prohibited.

### Insects

Visitors to the tropical rainforest are usually just as overwhelmed by the sounds of the 'jungle orchestra' as they are by the abundant vegetation. Composed of millions of insect noises, the hypnotic sound is so loud that it is easily heard even when passing through the forest in a car. By far the noisiest of the insects are male cicadas and grasshoppers, who produce their screeching and rasping sounds either by rubbing their wings together or by rubbing their leg against their wing.

The count of Malaysia's insect species grows every year as new discoveries are made. Butterflies number over 1,000 different varieties and moths an astonishing 8,000 species. The rainforest is said to have more butterflies per hectare than anywhere else on earth, and the ardent naturalist may well discover his or her very own species, as it is well known that the forest still holds many mysteries. Butterflies often gather on sandbanks by rivers, and the author was mesmerized one early morning beside a Perak river by the irridescent flashing of hundreds of the incomparable Rajah Brooke's Birdwings, with their dazzling bird-like wings daubed in metallic greens and black. Other butterflies are as fascinating as their names, such as the Dark Blue Jungle Glories, the Forest Nymphs, the Blue Wanderers, and the Great Mormons that swoop about like bats. In comparison, Malaysia's moths are rather drab, although just a few species are as colourful as butterflies. The largest of all is the Atlas Moth which can attain a wing span of 25 centimetres (10 inches).

Legions of other insects, too numerous to mention, and even too numerous to catalogue, inhabit every ecosystem of Malaysia. There are irridescent beetles, ants of all shapes and sizes, 700 different types of mosquitoes, poisonous centipedes, harmless millipedes, mantids and stick insects which are masters of disguise. There are bees, wasps and hornets, scorpions, spiders, and last, but not least, the voracious leech which is well known to anyone who has spent time in the forest.

## THE HISTORY OF MALAYSIA

### PREHISTORY

Theories have been tossed around for decades about Malaysia's earliest inhabitants. Scholars argued and debated over tenuous conjectures, and most textbooks on prehistory were out of date before they were even published. The million-year-old Java Man might have wandered through Malaysia on his way to Java, but this is mere speculation as no evidence has so far cropped up to support this assumption. Although it was accepted that a skull found in Sarawak's Niah Caves dated back to around 35,000 years ago, and evidence of human settlement at Baturong in Sabah was put at 30,000 years old, most archaeologists were at loggerheads over Peninsular Malaysia's Stone Age history: settlement here was generally believed to be much more recent than that in Malaysian Borneo. History books dated the first peopling of the Peninsula at approximately 10,000 years ago. However, a British archaeologist, Sieveking, and Walker, a geologist, had proposed the controversial theory that the Palaeolithic site of Kota Tampan in Perak was between 200,000 and half a million years old.

Deciding to try and solve once and for all the riddle of the Peninsula's Stone Age history, Malaysia's first woman archaeologist, Zuraina Majid, led an expeditionary team from Universiti Sains Malaysia in Penang to Kota Tampan in 1987. Their astounding findings were to change the prehistory of South-east Asia, for what they discovered was that this had been the site of a Stone Age workshop for making tools dating back to about 35,000 years ago. They found anvils and hammer-stones, and not only finished tools, but unfinished pieces and the debris and waste left over from the production. It was as though the workshop had been frozen in time, for not only was it undisturbed, but it was evident that some calamitous event had been responsible for an abrupt interruption. When Zuraina Majid analysed the soil around the workshop level the mystery was solved, for all the samples contained volcanic ash which chemically matched that from the final eruption of Sumatra's Lake Toba, around 31,000 years ago. As the ash from the massive blast blanketed the Peninsula, the workers must have abandoned the site. It had remained undisturbed until Zuraina Majid's team made their epic discovery. The missing link in Malaysia's prehistory had finally been forged.

It is theorized that in the Stone Age the climate was drier, forests more open and that the sea-level was a good 50 metres (165 feet) lower than it is today, which would have placed Kota Tampan much further inland and substantially altered the present coastline. About ten millennia ago, the climate warmed up and today's equatorial rainforests began to take over from the more open forests. Known as the Hoabinhian period, after an archaeological site in Vietnam, the lifestyle of early Malaysians who lived from 10,000 to 3,000 years ago is revealed by evidence found in limestone caves and shell-mounds both on the Peninsula and in Malaysian Borneo. Excavations at Kelantan's Gua Cha revealed that the Hoabinhians buried their dead in flexed positions, used flaked pebble tools, and ate a diet of shellfish, deer, pig, monkey, squirrel, and *seladang* (wild ox).

In Sabah, a similar society was discovered at the Madai caves, where intriguingly the site was abandoned around seven millennia ago and then re-established about 4,000 years later by a more advanced people who were making pottery and practising agriculture. Around the same time the Hoabinhians of Gua Cha were replaced by people that hunted with bone-pointed spears, and polished stone adzes, dressed themselves in bark-cloth clothing, bead necklaces and carved stone bracelets, and were adept at producing finely crafted pots. Times were also changing in Borneo; archaeological finds, including polished stone tools and even wooden coffins, from

*The Portuguese Gate, Melaka, in 1845, the last surviving remnant of the huge fort 'A Famosa' that once covered most of St Paul's Hill.*

Sarawak's Niah Caves showed that a more complex society had replaced the earlier one.

In West Malaysia, these Neolithic cultivators probably originated from Thailand and merely wandered down the Peninsula, bringing with them the knowledge of rice and millet growing, as their pottery is similar to that produced in central Thailand in the same era. Agricultural evidence, however, is scant as most of the limestone caves where prehistoric evidence has been found are now surrounded by rainforests, whereas in Thailand the early rice-growing sites are in more open land and are well documented.

Who the early peoples were, and where they came from, is still the subject of debates and disagreements between archaeologists and anthropologists. However, Peter Bellwood, probably the best qualified expert on the subject and the author of *Prehistory of the Indo-Malaysian Archipelago*, is of the opinion that the Semang (or Negritos) of the Peninsula's northern forests are the direct descendants of the Hoabinhians. Numbering around 2,000, these formerly nomadic hunter-gatherers have dark skins, curly hair, and are shorter than the other Peninsular peoples. Bellwood also believes that the Senoi, whose name literally means 'human being', are possibly the descendants of the Hoabinhians and the Neolithic cultivators who arrived in the Malay Peninsula from southern Thailand around 2,000 BC. These Orang Asli cultivators, numbering around 40,000, live in the inland, forested parts of Perak, Pahang and Kelantan. Both the Semang and the Senoi speak a Mon-Khmer dialect similar to that of Kampuchea's Khmer and Vietnamese.

Sometime between 500 BC and AD 500 the Peninsula underwent an enormous change. This Stone Age land was infiltrated by people who, according to evidence unearthed from archaeological digs, used iron tools, and bronze drums known as Dongson, after the place in Vietnam where they were manufactured. These people were the ancestors of today's Malays and other Austronesian-speaking groups, like the present Orang Asli, who speak Malay-type languages. Probably originating from southern China or Taiwan, the Malays filtered through maritime South-east Asia, from the Philippines, through eastern Indonesia, Borneo, Sumatra, and finally to the Malay Peninsula. The Malay colonization was so widespread that today they are probably the most far-flung of all the earth's major ethnolinguistic groups, stretching across the Indian Ocean to Madagascar, embracing most of South-east Asia and continuing across the Pacific to encompass all of Oceania beyond western Melanesia.

## EARLY HISTORY

### Legendary Malay Kingdoms

A mere glance at the position of the Malay archipelago on a world map is enough to enable even the least expert geographer to understand why this area has for at least two millennia been at the heart of the great Asiatic trading routes. Arab dhows and Indian merchant ships were blown across the Indian Ocean until they met the protruding Malay Peninsula, a natural barrier between East and West Asia. They were then forced into the funnel of the Straits of Melaka which brought them to the Spice Islands, now Indonesia, in the east, unless they changed tack and sailed north to China.

There are plentiful legends, but little tangible evidence of the dozens of Malay kingdoms which flourished from the fifth century until the emergence of Melaka in the late 14th century. Before the sixth century, when a major trade route flourished across the Isthmus of Kra in southern Thailand, Funan, in what is now Kampuchea, was the centre of mainland power, controlling many minor kingdoms in Peninsular Malaysia. But when the sea routes were popularized other maritime kingdoms evolved. Melayu in Sumatra was sited near modern Jambi, and the influential Srivijaya, the precursor of Melaka, was probably situated on Sumatra's east coast, although dissident scholars have even suggested the north-east of the Malay Peninsula. This powerful kingdom, which exercised imperial control over all East-West trade, forced shipping through the Melaka Straits. Tolls and tribute were exacted by the ports and other kingdoms which were under the suzerainty of Srivijaya.

Known to Greek geographers as 'The Golden Khersonese' and to the Indians as 'The Land of Gold', the Malay Peninsula had a well-founded reputation as a region where gold was plentiful, even though it is not found in great quantities today. The location of Marco Polo's enigmatic Lokak 'a large and wealthy province of the mainland', where 'gold is so plentiful that no one who did not see it could believe it', has never been established, but it could easily have been in the north-east of Peninsular Malaysia. He tells of 'elephants and wild game in profusion', and that from this kingdom 'come all the cowrie shells that are spent in all the provinces of which I have told you'. On leaving Lokak, Marco Polo sailed on to Bintan Island 'southwards for 500 miles'. Kota Bharu, the present-day capital of Kelantan state, is roughly the same distance from Bintan, given the Venetian adventurer's rough-and-ready ideas of geography, and could easily have been Lokak. This vicinity, including Thailand's Pattani, which was a Malay sultanate until this century, was also the probable site of two legendary kingdoms which existed for at least five centuries before Marco Polo sailed the South China Sea.

Of these early trading kingdoms there are no tangible remains, only literary references. Chinese mariners' guides, Arab sailors' tales, and diaries by Buddhist pilgrims *en route* to India, all tell of such ancient trading kingdoms. There was Langkasuka, famed for its camphor-wood, which according to a sixth-century Chinese account took a month to cross from east to west. Bedecked in gold jewellery, the king and his nobles lived in a walled city, and travelled abroad on elephant-back, shaded by white howdahs and escorted by drummers, soldiers and followers carrying fans and banners.

Another legendary kingdom, known to the Chinese as Chih Tu, The Lion City, capital of the 'red earth land' of Kelantan, was located a month's journey inland. Visiting seventh-century envoys told how the monarch's ocean-going fleets carried the kingdom's gold, camphor, and other rainforest bounty to overseas markets.

On the other side of the Peninsula, Gunung Jerai, a 1,330 metre (4,630 feet) peak on Kedah's seaboard, was an obvious beacon for mariners journeying across the

Bay of Bengal. On its south-west slopes archaeologists have discovered dozens of Buddhist and Hindu temple remnants dating from the fifth century. They are not spectacular ruins, being mainly sandstone and brick temple platforms, but they are a fascinating link with the past as they are tangible reminders of Malaysia's pre-Islamic past. Tamil traders knew old Kedah as Katahara, and a seventh-century Sanskrit drama describes it as Katha. Kedah began as a prehistoric Malay settlement at Sungai Muda, becoming an important landfall for Indian shipping and then evolving into an entrepôt by the mid-seventh century. Buddhist images and inscriptions, obviously Indian inspired, date from the fifth century, but toward the end of the ninth century the port of Pengkalan Bujang rose to prominence and Hindu temples then predominated. Although Hinduism died out with the coming of Islam in the 14th century, Indian influence in the Malay way of life, even today, is enormous. Court ritual, wedding traditions, hundreds of everyday words, epic tales, vital cooking ingredients, are but some of the pervasive influences that India has contributed.

### The Rise and Fall of Melaka

It seems that the older a city is, the more fanciful are the legends that surround its birth, and Melaka, which recently celebrated its 600th birthday, is no exception. Its meteoric rise as the supreme kingdom of the Malays was no accident, however: Parameswara, its founder, boasted an impeccable pedigree which could be traced back to the rulers of Palembang in Sumatra, through Indian dynasties to Alexander the Great, known to the Muslims as Raja Iskandar. After being forced to flee Singapura (ancient Singapore) when the Javanese attacked, Parameswara journeyed to Muar on the Melaka Straits. The legend has it that one day while journeying north with a hunting party his royal dogs were intimidated by a courageous mouse-deer, which was considered an auspicious sign (apparently Chiangmai in Thailand was founded after a similar occurrence). It so impressed the Sumatran prince that he decided to found a new kingdom on the site, which he named Melaka after the tree under which he was resting.

*The beach at Melaka, around 1900. The coastline here has since disappeared under housing estates built on reclaimed land, but relics of Melaka's rich history can still be found in the centre of the old city.*

Situated on the strategic Straits, Melaka quickly rose to prominence. Its monarch's regal connections ensured that the sea-tribes, known as Orang Laut, paid allegiance to him, thus guaranteeing that the surrounding waters were pirate free. In 1403, probably only a decade after its foundation, Chinese envoys sailed into the harbour laden with silks, and three years later the emperor recognized Parameswara as Sultan of Melaka and accorded the port the right to be the 'sole distributor' of Chinese goods, guaranteeing its success. Dominant among the traders were the wealthy Muslim Indians whose religion commanded considerable prestige. The fact that they flocked to Muslim ports, including Melaka's competitors in Sumatra, would certainly have been considered by Parameswara when he converted to Islam early in the 15th century to become the first Sultan of Melaka. He was not the first Muslim ruler of Malaysia, however. A stone tablet found upriver from Kuala Terengganu is inscribed with Islamic rules proclaimed by Raja Mandulika at least 25 years before Melaka's conversion.

The 'Three-Jewelled Eunuch', otherwise known as the Muslim Commander of the Imperial Ming Fleet, Admiral Cheng Ho, made seven voyages to Melaka between 1405 and 1431. According to historical sources his 50-strong fleet of 48-metre-long (160 feet) wooden junks carried an astonishing 37,000 soldiers. Asian monarchs had no qualms about paying tribute to the Chinese for they brought plentiful trade. In addition, they provided protection against the Thais who also demanded tribute, but unlike the Chinese brought no trade.

Overlooking the harbour, on the hill later known as St Paul's, the sultans and their court enjoyed a lavish lifestyle. Rulers enjoyed absolute power and undivided loyalty from their subjects. The concept of *daulat*, a type of mystical kingly power, placed the sultan above society and criticism. Accordingly, the crime of *derhaka*, or treason, was punishable, according to the *Sejarah Melayu*, the court annals of the Melakan sultanate, by killing not only the guilty party, but his entire family. In addition, the perpetrator's house would be uprooted and the soil it stood on thrown into the sea. However, the annals also warned that rulers would not succeed unless they listened to the advice of their ministers, and some of these attained fame to rival even that of their sultans. Tun Perak, who was Prime Minister, or *bendahara*, for four decades of Melaka's century of power, was the real power behind the throne, and during his tenure Melaka became the most influential and prosperous state in South-east Asia.

Sultan Mansur Shah's reign (1459-1477) marked the pinnacle of Malay power and culture. The *Sejarah Melayu* recounts the legendary happenings, intrigues, and scandals of this Golden Age. During this time the famous Orang Laut, Hang Tuah, rose from obscurity to become the Laksamana, the Admiral of the Fleet, and tales of his derring-do and strikingly handsome appearance enliven the pages of the Annals. Apparently he caused such a sensation whenever he went abroad that even 'married women tore themselves from the embraces of their husbands, so they could go and see him'.

Sultan Mansur Shah's successor, Sultan Alau'd-din Riayat Shah, was a keen administrator, and extended Melaka's boundaries to include most of the Malay Peninsula, the Sumatran coast, and countless islands in between. However, after such an auspicious beginning his reign was abruptly terminated by suspected poisoning when he was only 26. After Alau'd-din's death in 1488, the youthful Sultan Mahmud Shah took the throne. According to the author of the *Sejarah Melayu* he was cruel, tyrannical and debauched, but the writer did happen to be the nephew of the Bendahara that Mahmud had executed, so Malay history could have been tainted by his bias. However, Bendahara Mutahir could hardly have endeared himself to the young sultan by his blatant flaunting of his fortune. Boasting of his wealth to Melaka's merchants, Mutahir often changed his outfit several times a day and was reputed to own a thousand jackets.

Melaka at the beginning of the 16th century was at the zenith of its power, a cosmopolitan city with a population of 100,000 where scores of languages were spoken in the street. The economy of this fascinating, exotic hub of the kingdom rested entirely in its entrepôt trade. Merchants from Persia, Arabia, Asia Minor and East Africa shipped 30 different types of cloth, rose-water, opium, incense and grains. The Gujerati, Tamil and Bengali traders from the Indian sub-continent bartered cloth and the tails of white Bengal cattle for cloves. The Burmese, Thais, Javanese, Bugis, Minangkabau, and Malays of South-east Asia dealt in nutmegs, mace, camphor, sandalwood, musk, batik, Javanese *keris*, tin, bird-plumes, rhinoceros horn, tortoiseshell, rubies and other exotica, while the Chinese filled their junks with silks, satins, seed pearls, musk, camphor, sulphur, copper, ironware, trinkets, drugs, ivory and ebony.

Across the South China Sea on the great jungled isle of Borneo, two other entrepôts, namely, Po-ni, probably the precursor of today's sultanate of Brunei, and Vijayapura, which was situated somewhere on the west coast, had been centres of trade for centuries prior to the rise of Melaka. Indian Buddhist relics found in the Sarawak delta date from the sixth century and Ming pottery from the 13th century discovered in the same area indicates that this was also an important trading port. Islam probably came to Po-ni from Melaka, and with the conversion Brunei was considered as being within the ambience of the Malay world. However, apart from Brunei, little is known of the early history of Sabah and Sarawak.

By the end of the 15th century Melaka was, in the words of the Portuguese historian, Duarte Barbosa, 'the richest sea port with the greatest number of wholesale merchants and abundance of shipping that can be found in the whole world'. However, it was precisely the factors that had realized Melaka's wealth which led to her undoing. Tales of this wondrous city had been filtering back to Europe, and the Portuguese were convinced that in order to overtake Arab domination of the spice trade they had to conquer Melaka. For the power that ruled the Straits also controlled the spice market in Europe.

When the first Portuguese expedition, commanded by Diogo Lopes de Sequeira, anchored at Melaka in 1509, the 'White Bengalis' initially fascinated the Malays. Their interest soon turned to distaste, however, when, after presenting their petition to trade, the Portuguese placed a necklace around the Bendahara's neck with their own hands. This gross breach of court etiquette convinced the Malays that the Portuguese were a race of ill-mannered boors. In addition, Melaka's Muslim-Indian traders had already experienced Portuguese competition in India and were less than enthusiastic over this European foray into the East, so they persuaded the Bendahara to eliminate the Portuguese with a surprise night attack. However, the plot misfired when a Javanese girl swam out and warned her Portuguese lover. Sequeira was forced to head back to India leaving 20 of his crew stranded.

Nevertheless, the Portuguese timing was impeccable. The court was riddled with factionalism and the powerful Bendahara whom Sultan Mahmud had executed had been replaced by a powerless puppet. When Alfonso de Albuquerque, the governor of Portuguese India, arrived in 1511 he demanded the release of the Portuguese prisoners and requested permission to build a trading post. His requests fell on deaf ears so he blockaded the harbour and began his attack. Although the Malays fought valiantly the Portuguese persisted with their superior firepower. The Melakans were astonished by cannon balls that fell like rain: 'What may be this round weapon that yet is sharp enough to kill us?'

After pages devoted to the bravery of the Melaka Malays in their skirmishes and battles with the Portuguese, the *Sejarah Melayu* has but three words to describe the last stand of the greatest Malay kingdom of all time: 'And Melaka fell.' It would be four and a half centuries before the city would return to Malay rule.

## THE COLONIAL ERA

### The Coming of the Europeans

When Albuquerque and his conquering army marched five abreast through the streets of Melaka, the sultan and his court had already fled overland to Pahang and from there to Bintan in the Riau-Lingga archipelago south of Singapore. Backed by a formidable navy of Orang Laut, the regional sea-tribes, the former dynasty launched numerous attacks on Melaka and the Portuguese responded by counter-attacking their new southern base. When the exiled sultan died in 1528, his son, Alauddin Riayat Shah, established his court at Pekan Tua on the Johor River and became the first ruler of what was later to become the kingdom of Johor. The former rulers of Melaka gave substantial aid to the Dutch when they recaptured the city in 1640, although their trust was misplaced for Melaka stayed in foreign hands.

'Whoever is lord of Melaka has his hand on the throat of Venice,' is one of Tomé Pires' most quoted maxims, for in the early 16th century the Venetians controlled the European end of the spice trade. But after the euphoria of conquest, the reality of dominating the Straits trade proved a pipe-dream. Vital Muslim trade defected to Aceh in Sumatra, and Portugal's rapid colonial expansion and mounting debts from wars in India, as well as numerous sieges and attacks on Melaka, depleted the Portuguese coffers. Their influence was confined to the Melakan region and later reports suggest that although the Portuguese built a fine fortified city, 'with big houses of wood or stone and very narrow and regular streets after the Portuguese style,' Melaka's heyday was over.

In 1641, after a five-month siege which reduced the city's population from 20,000 to 7,000 inhabitants, the Dutch East India Company achieved a bittersweet victory. Melaka was ruined, but the conquerors were undeterred and proceeded to rebuild Melaka in the image of a Dutch trading town. Keen to cash in on the profitable tin trade, the Dutch were eager to draw up monopoly trade agreements with the Malays, who in turn wanted military assistance against the Acehnese and the Siamese. But when such help was called on, the Dutch were lax to keep their side of the bargain. They were already looking further afield to Batavia, their new spice port in Java, for most of their profits.

Under the rule of the heirs to the powerful Melakan dynasty, Johor rose to prominence in the 17th century, and according to a Malay history, *Tuhfat al-Nafis*, 'The Precious Gift', the kingdom 'prospered, and was famed not only for the refinement of its customs, but also for its culture'. Johoreans are still renowned for these qualities three centuries later. By the end of the century the Johor empire encompassed Selangor, Pahang, Terengganu, and even Siak in Sumatra, but in 1699 an event occurred which had a momentous effect on the entire Malay world and the course of history. When the heirless Sultan Mahmud was murdered by his nobles the great dynasty of the 'white-blooded' rulers of Melaka came to an end. Although by all accounts he was corrupt, cruel and incompetent, he was still, according to Malay legends, the last direct descendant of Alexander the Great, and the regicide was bitterly condemned.

Elsewhere, the present-day states of the Peninsula were gradually emerging as sovereign units in their own right. Kedah, Pattani (now in Thailand), and Kelantan were ruled by their own sultans, though they paid tribute to and were under the authority of the Thai court. Tin-rich Perak made trade agreements with the Dutch and enjoyed an unprecedented era of peace known ever since as Perak's 'Golden Age'. Meanwhile, Bugis and Makassarese, who had fled the civil war raging in their Sulawesi homeland, were settling along the Selangor coast. By 1717 the Bugis had already taken control of the Johor court. Later in the century, Terengganu shrugged off Johor's colonial yoke and became an independent state.

### British Malaya

In 1786, with the backing of the English East India Company, the adventurous Englishman, Captain Francis Light, talked the Sultan of Kedah into signing over the island of Penang. In return, the Malay ruler expected support against his enemies, the Thais, but he soon found out that this was not in the imperial scheme of things. He blockaded the island in 1790, but his forces had little chance of success against the might of the British Empire.

The British had already gained control of the Indian cloth and opium markets, and needed a port to refit their clippers *en route* to China in pursuit of the lucrative tea trade. Initially Penang thrived: traders rushed to take advantage of the new tax- and duty-free port – a British strategy to lure trade away from the Dutch ports. Chinese, Indians, Arabs, and traders from the vast Malay Archipelago flocked to 'the Pearl of the Orient'. When Sir Stamford Raffles established Singapore in 1819, Penang's importance declined, but the British push into the Peninsula was just beginning. The booming British-run ports effectively siphoned off the trade of the Malay-run ports. In 1824 the Malay world suffered another crippling blow when the Anglo-Dutch Treaty of London severed its cultural unity. The Riau-Lingga Archipelago, traditionally the fief of the Sultanate of Johor, was given to the Dutch, and access to Sumatra, legendary homeland of the Malay rulers and their language, was denied to the Malays of the Peninsula. Two years later, the British took control of the Straits Settlements which included Penang, the mainland province opposite known as Province Wellesley, Melaka and Singapore.

Politically, the Peninsula was undergoing enormous changes, but even more momentous were the demographic alterations. Chinese immigrants fleeing from appalling conditions in their homeland were pouring in to work the tin mines and establish agricultural plantations. Gradually, under the guise of helping to settle dynastic disputes and Chinese secret society wars which had destabilized the lucrative tin business, the

*The Market, Johor Bahru, in 1910. The town, whose name means 'new Johor', was established as his capital by Sultan Abu Bakar in 1866.*

*Sultan Abu Bakar of Johor in 1891. Regarded as the father of modern Johor, the anglophile Abu Bakar had received an English education in Singapore and made several visits to the British court, but took care to remain independent of British rule.*

British made their advance into the interior. They persuaded the Malay chiefs to accept British Residents, who would keep the peace but not interfere with Malay law and religion. But Malay rule by British advice was exposed as fiction in 1875 when the Resident of Perak, J. W. W. Birch, posted notices of a controversial new enactment giving the British control of judicial affairs. He was murdered while pinning them up. His killers were hanged and others exiled, but later they were to be recognized as having been among the first Malay nationalists. However, by 1888, Negeri Sembilan, Selangor, and Pahang had all signed treaties to accept Residents. Only six years earlier an British surveyor had been refused admittance to Negeri Sembilan because he was prophetically told: 'If we let the needle in, the thread is sure to follow.'

In 1896 the Federated Malay States (FMS), a British protectorate headed by a British High Commissioner, was formed. It consisted of Negeri Sembilan, Pahang, Perak and Selangor, with Kuala Lumpur as its capital. Although he was an intimate of Queen Victoria, Johor's Sultan Abu Bakar had adroitly introduced a constitution prohibiting alignment with European powers, enabling his state to retain its sovereignty. However, his heir was not as clever at keeping the hounds at bay. When Britain concluded a treaty with Siam ceding Kedah, Kelantan, and Terengganu to the British in return for diplomatic privileges, the indignant ruler of Kedah announced that his country 'had been bought and sold like a buffalo', and the outraged Sultan of Terengganu accused the Thais of bargaining with stolen property. By 1919 the Union Jack fluttered over every state on the Malay Peninsula. 'British Malaya' was complete.

### Sarawak's 'White Rajahs' and British North Borneo

James Brooke, an adventurous Indian-born Englishman, was fascinated with Borneo and had long cradled similar ambitions to Singapore's Sir Stamford Raffles. As Brooke was intending to sail his schooner *The Royalist* across to North Borneo, the governor of Singapore entrusted him with a message for the Raja Muda of Brunei. As luck would have it, Brooke arrived just in time to help the Raja quell a rebellion, and as a reward he was given a large chunk of Sarawak as his personal fief. In 1841 Brooke set up his capital at Kuching on the Sarawak River, establishing a remarkable dynasty that was to rule Sarawak for the next century. The self-styled 'White Rajah' quickly won over the peaceful Bidayuhs. In keeping with his hero Raffles' idea of a benevolent administration which would protect the trader while fostering native welfare, he pardoned the local Malays who had troubled the Raja and gave them administrative positions in his government. The Iban, renowned for their head-hunting and warlike ways, were not as easily subdued, but with masterly guile Brooke launched an anti-piracy campaign. All Iban raids were thereafter called piracy and this proved an excellent method of extending his territories as he recruited Iban allies. In 1853 Brunei transferred the formerly Iban-controlled areas to Brooke in return for an annual rental of £1,500.

*James Brooke, the first 'White Rajah' of Sarawak, in 1848.*

If businessmen had thought that Sarawak's English rajah would open the floodgates of commerce into Borneo they were to be sadly disillusioned. Brooke was against Western commercialism, mainly because of the effect it would have on the indigenous culture. In the early days of Brooke rule London was reluctant to grant Sarawak a formal protectorate. However, as other colonial powers like France began moving into South-east Asia, the prospect of having another British post on the South China Sea looked more appealing. In 1863 a British consul was appointed, effectively recognizing that Sarawak was a separate entity from Brunei. This association helped to reinforce the connection with the Malay Peninsula and as Charles Brooke, the second Rajah of Sarawak, said, 'Wherever the Sarawak flag is planted, there English interests will be paramount.' Slowly the boundaries of modern Malaysia were being refined.

Brunei had exercised nominal power over North Borneo for centuries, although in 1704 the sultans of Sulu, who had helped the Sultan of Brunei in a succession dispute, were given the land east of Marudu Bay, in much the same way that James Brooke later secured his fief. The powerful Sulu empire was ruled from the island of Jolo, in

*His Royal Highness Sri Paduka Al Sultan Mohamet Jamal Al Alam bin Sri Paduka Al Marhom Al Sultan Mohomet Fathlon, Sultan of Sulu, seated between William Clarke Cowie (centre of picture), first managing director of the British North Borneo Chartered Company, and the company's treasurer Mr A Cook. The company received its royal charter in 1881, three years after the sultan had ceded to it the territory which formed most of present-day Sabah.*

what is now the southern Philippines. Two and a half centuries later, history came back to haunt Malaysia when the Philippines laid claim to this sizeable portion of Sabah, as the state is now called, and the dispute is still being waged.

In the mid-19th century the British started developing an interest in northern Borneo, mainly because they were worried that Spain might try to enlarge her empire southwards from the Philippines. By this time Brunei's control over the north coast of Borneo was tenuous to say the least and the sultan was easily persuaded to lease most of present-day Sabah to an adventuring American by the name of Lee Moses. He sold the rights to the American Trading Company, which caused such distress in London that official checks were made with Washington, but the United States allayed any fears by stressing that the government had no official connections with the lessees. In 1877 Baron Gustav von Overbeck, the Austrian Consul-General in Hong Kong, purchased the lease, ostensibly with capital from an Englishman, Alfred Dent. Overbeck secured an agreement with the Sultan of Brunei for the cession of the territory in return for an annual payment of 15,000 Straits dollars. Then, discovering that the Sultan of Sulu was the actual ruler of the territory, he visited him to negotiate a further lease in return for an annual sum of 5,000 Straits dollars. With the aid of his influential London contacts Dent succeeded in obtaining a royal charter three years later and formed the British North Borneo Company in 1881. A condition of the charter was that the company should be entirely British-owned, and Baron von Overbeck was forced to sell his share. From then, until the Japanese conquest 60 years later, the Company ruled the state known as British North Borneo, although the country continued to be known by its indigenous inhabitants, and the Bruneians, as Sabah.

In comparison with the effective management of Sarawak, Sabah's economy in those early days merely limped along, and for the first decade of its existence bankruptcy was an everyday spectre. The administrators boasted that they had abolished slavery and stamped out head-hunting, but most of the benefits of colonial life did not extend beyond the towns. Collecting taxes was never easy and as the historian Barbara Watson-Andaya wrote, 'Without a personality like Brooke, and without access to a fighting force like the Ibans, the Company found the collection of taxes difficult.' Their rigidity was a problem, as a Bajau of that time remarked: 'Although the Bruneians fined people hundreds of piculs it was all mere words and they can give what they have, but the white man's two dollars is two dollars and no less.'

It was probably the taxes that incited Mat Salleh, a Sulu prince, to declare war on the Company in 1895. This charismatic leader was said to have a genius for military

*The Sarawak Railway, opened in 1915, was a project in which Rajah Charles Brooke took great pride, but it was not a success and its track, running south of Kuching, never exceeded 10 miles in length.*

affairs, and to possess considerable mystical powers and great physical strength. As a youth he was said to be capable of throwing a buffalo by its horns. When the British administrator William Cowie met him he was struck by his appearance, saying, 'His manner and appearance made me aware that I was face to face with the Rob Roy of British North Borneo.' Mat Salleh certainly led the British a merry dance until he was killed in 1900, although his followers waged guerrilla war for another five years. In colonial days schoolchildren were told he was a troublemaker, but these days he is a national hero.

## MODERN HISTORY: BEFORE AND AFTER INDEPENDENCE

### The Push for Independence

Although the colonial administration perpetuated the myth that Malaya belonged to the Malays and that the immigrant ethnic groups were merely transients who were extracting the Peninsula's riches for the ultimate welfare of its own people, the reality was quite different. Pursuing a 'divide and rule' policy, the British had encouraged the Malays into government while leaving commerce to the Chinese, a legacy which is still strikingly evident in today's Malaysia, despite attempts to balance the situation. In 1903 only a few thousand Malays were employed by the Federated Malay States (FMS) government, and these were mainly policemen. However, the situation was entirely different in Johor and the formerly Thai-controlled states, where Malays still managed their own affairs.

As a result of demands for English education the Malay College at Kuala Kangsar opened, ostensibly for the sons of the nobility. It soon gained the nickname of 'Bab ud-Darajat' – The Gateway to High Rank – for the graduates were quickly absorbed into the public service and European commercial enterprises, which offered the prize of *gaji bulan*, a steady monthly salary.

*A view of Kuala Lumpur in about 1900, shortly after it had become capital of the Federated Malay States.*

Naturally, the colonial administration were reluctant to provide the masses with any more than basic schooling, as an educated class would obviously see shortcomings in the system and begin to question where they, the Malays, stood in the changing society. However, this was exactly what happened. Teachers, who mainly trained in Egypt, were bringing home notions of Islamic reform, while the Chinese were forced to rethink their role in Malaya when their homeland was undergoing such revolutionary changes.

### The Japanese Occupation

Meanwhile, the colonial administrators went on living in a time-warp until they were rudely awakened by the Japanese invasion in

December 1941. While seemingly impregnable Singapore watched the sea, the Japanese landed at Kota Bharu in the far north-east of the Peninsula, and swarmed overland. A land attack had hardly been considered, and as Colonel Spenser Chapman recalled, 'Nor had the natives of the country been in any way prepared to expect or resist invasion. There was no united front.' By February 1942 the Japanese had taken all Malaya, Singapore, and even Borneo. Europeans were rounded up and taken to prison camps. Thousands died, especially those who were shipped north to build the notorious Burma railway, and in the infamous Death March when prisoners of war were forced to march from Sandakan to Ranau in Sabah. Because of their recent war with China, the Japanese vented their anger at the Chinese community in Malaya and many escaped death by joining resistance groups like the Malayan Communist Party (MCP) which dominated the guerrilla war in the jungle. Adopting the slogan 'Asia for Asians', the Japanese anxiously wooed the Malays and the Indians.

Although in the early years of their occupation the Japanese were primarily interested in Malaya's economic contribution to the war, when the tide began to turn they increasingly played up the need for Malay nationalism. This was already a growing force among the educated elite, but was also now gaining grass-roots support. The seemingly indestructible British Empire had been humiliated by its defeat, and even after the Japanese surrendered and the colonial administration once again took up the reins, its inheritance was tenuous to say the least.

### Independence

Impressed by the Chinese role in wartime resistance, the British came up with a plan for the Malayan Union which more than anything else demonstrated how out of touch they were with the current situation of the Malays. They proposed to give Chinese and Indians equal citizenship, while the sultans' sovereignty would be transferred to the British Crown. They were taken aback when the Malays, who they had always considered to be apathetic, violently objected, and formed the United Malays National Organisation (UMNO) which gave special privileges to the Malays and upheld the status of the sultans. In 1948 the unpopular Malayan Union was thrown out and was replaced by the Federation of Malaya. Its constitution gave the sultans power over their respective states and reserved the special status of Malays as the original occupants of the Peninsula. In the same year the British also committed themselves to prepare the way for Independence, but plans were put on hold when the communist guerrillas, whose ranks had been swelled with disenchanted Chinese, embarked on a terror campaign against the British. The Malayan Emergency, as it was called, officially ended only in 1960, but its first years were the most successful. Under their charismatic leader, Chin Peng, the communists murdered and harassed European planters and mining officials. When they killed the British High Commissioner in 1951 the administration was forced into accelerated action. The communists' tactics were undermined by the vigorous implementation of a policy launched in 1950, by which rural Chinese communities were relocated into 'new villages' where they were under surveillance and subject to curfews. This arrangement made it difficult for sympathizers to provide food and assistance to the guerrillas. The insurgents were forced deeper into the jungle and by the time the Malayan Chinese Association (MCA) and the Malayan Indian Congress (MIC) joined with UMNO to form the Alliance the communists were seen as an impotent force. Small bands continued to wage a guerrilla war, however, and only surrendered in 1992. When the multi-ethnic, and pro-independence Alliance won an overwhelming majority at the 1955 election, the machinery was set in motion to grant Malaya independence. Two years later, on 15 August, 1957, Britain relinquished its sovereignty, and the first Prime Minister, Tunku Abdul Rahman, declared Malaya independent.

### After Independence

*'Merdeka'*, the cry for freedom, echoed over the land, but ethnic divisions, a direct legacy of the British 'divide and rule' policy, were to be the new government's biggest bugbear. In 1963, when Singapore, Sabah, and Sarawak joined with Malaya to form Malaysia, the nation not only doubled its geographical size, but inherited the huge Chinese population of Singapore plus the multi-ethnic races of Borneo. Cultural polity became an even more delicate balancing act. Added to this problem was the outrage of neighbouring countries over the formation of Malaysia. The Philippines claimed Sabah as part of the Sulu sultanate, and Indonesia launched its *Konfrontasi*, a campaign of confrontation against Malaysia which came perilously close to war. Meanwhile, Singapore pressed for a more egalitarian policy, but the Tunku was alarmed at recent race riots in Singapore and decided that to avoid worse ethnic conflicts Malaysia and Singapore should separate. In 1965 the island nation of Singapore became a republic.

When President Sukarno was ousted in 1966, Indonesia made peace with Malaysia, but trouble was growing on the home front. Communal violence broke out after the 1969 elections when the Alliance lost a number of seats and control of two states. After four days of violent clashes, known ever since as the Riots of 13 May, parliament was suspended and Tun Abdul Razak ran the country under emergency rule until he was elected as Prime Minister of the newly convened parliament in 1971. In the wake of the troubles, national ideologies were formed and educational policies, with Malay as the medium, were set in motion. Programmes designed to eradicate poverty, such as the New Economic Policy (NEP), significantly improved the position of the rural Malays.

The prosperous 1970s enabled Tun Abdul Razak and his successor, Tun Hussein Onn, to make considerable economic progress. The ruling coalition, now known as the *Barisan Nasional* (BN), which also encompassed parties from Sabah and Sarawak, retained parliamentary majorities and effectively coped with the problems of the decade.

Malaysia's economic and political status accelerated in the 1980s, led by Dato' Seri Dr Mahathir bin Mohamad, Malaysia's fourth Prime Minister. He initiated the 'Look East' policy which searched for new sources of support and development, and a bold and hugely successful policy of heavy industrialization which saw the production of the national car and the development of the steel industry and oil refineries. Once sacked from UMNO for criticizing the Tunku, and renowned for his forthright and authoritarian style, Mahathir is not without his critics. His tactics to silence the judiciary, remove his opponents, gag the press, and limit the powers of the traditional rulers have all come under fire. However, after narrowly surviving a challenge to his party leadership, Mahathir went on to an impressive win in the 1990 election.

With a booming economy, and the projection that the nation will attain the status of a developed country by 2020, Malaysia is firmly on the road to prosperity. Although its communal problems have still not been solved, the nation is now looking towards a wider perspective. In comparison with other countries where ethnic violence is growing, Malaysia is a model of racial harmony, an indication of the maturity that the country has achieved in only 30 years since independence.

## PEOPLES OF MALAYSIA

Pion Anak Bumbon spends most days behind his house, where it is coolest. Shaded by a canopy of fruit trees and cocoa bushes, the master-craftsman of the Mah Meri sits lotus-style on a carpet of rose-coloured wood chips while he carves his 'spirit' sculptures. 'Our women,' he explains, 'are not allowed to walk here when they are pregnant, as we believe that this may cause the unborn child to be born with features like the spirit which is being carved.' Known as *moyang*, which loosely translates as 'ancestor', the wooden sculptures are based on the pantheon of Mah Meri spirit-deities which form the basis of their animist beliefs. These are invariably bound up in their traditional environment – the swamp, the forest and the sea. Pion, like all the elders, believes that the Mah Meri, a sub-branch of the Senoi who speak a Mon-Khmer dialect, originally emigrated from Johor to their island home off the Selangor coast. He has no idea when they made the move, however. As for most of Malaysia's original people, these migrations are part of their oral history, which reaches back into the mists of time.

Numbering around 1,400, the Mah Meri are but one of about 20 different Peninsular groups with a combined population of at least 90,000, known collectively as the Orang Asli, or 'original people'. They are regarded by government classification as being part of the *bumiputra* (sons of the soil) category, as are the Malays, the Malay-related groups like the Bugis and Minangkabau, and the original ethnic groups of Sabah and Sarawak. The non-*bumiputra* groups consist mainly of later immigrant peoples like the Chinese and Indians, and smaller communities like the Eurasians and Arabs.

### ORANG ASLI – THE ORIGINAL PEOPLE

Before the Malays arrived, probably around two millennia ago, the Malay Peninsula was peopled by nomadic hunters and gatherers, and other tribes that practised slash-and-burn agriculture. Where these people came from is still a matter of conjecture, but the best clues come from studying their languages. These days, it is supposed that the Orang Asli who speak a Mon-Khmer dialect like that of Kampuchea and Vietnam were the first arrivals, and those who speak Malay-related languages came later.

Without question, Malaysia's oldest people are the Semang, previously dubbed the Negritos, who, until recently, lived a nomadic life deep in the northern rainforests. They are found in the highlands of Kelantan, Terengganu, and the northern regions of Perak, Kedah, and Pahang. With a population of around 2,000 – a figure unchanged for a century – the Semang comprise six different sub-groups: the Batek, Jahai, Kensiu, Kintak, Lanoh and Mendrik. Muscular, small of stature, with darker skin and curlier hair than the other Peninsular peoples, the Negritos were long thought to be related to Andaman islanders and aboriginals of the Philippines. These days, however, scholars think that they could be the descendants of other Orang Asli groups, and that their physical differences came about through thousands of years of adaptation to their rainforest home. Naturally, after millennia of forest life, the Semang are masters of their environment. Even though many now live a semi-settled existence, some still retain their former nomadic lifestyle. Roaming in groups numbering no more than 30 people, the women would gather yams, berries, nuts, fruit and leaves, while the men would snare or trap larger animals like deer, wild pigs or tapirs, or hunt smaller game like monkeys, squirrels and birds with bows and arrows – their traditional weapons – or by using blowpipes which they adopted from the Senoi. Their temporary shelters were made utilizing large leaves as a roof which was supported by poles; the floors were constructed of split bamboo. Never having practised even basic cultivation, the Semang were the original conservationists. Living a totally organic existence, they made practically no impact on their rainforest environment. As Charles Shuttleworth wrote of the Semang in his *Jungle Dwellers of the Malay Peninsula*: 'He is the true child of the rain forests, nature's own gentleman.'

The Senoi were originally dubbed 'Sakai', a derogatory Malay term which means 'inferior'. The name Senoi translates as 'human being', and this group is the most populous of all Orang Asli, numbering around 40,000. Archaeological evidence suggests that they arrived later than the Semang, but their dialects have the same Mon-Khmer roots. Physically they are quite different, being slightly taller, and having paler skin and wavy hair. Their lifestyles were also dissimilar as the Senoi were adept at swidden agriculture (shifting cultivation) as well as fishing, trapping, hunting, and gathering rainforest products. Their blowpipe skills are legendary. Intricately carved and measuring over two metres (six feet) long, bamboo blowpipes are deadly accurate up to at least eight metres (nine yards). These days the Senoi also cultivate rubber, fruit crops, and cocoa, and many have entered mainstream Malaysian life. Of the various Senoi groups who live in upland Kelantan, Perak, Pahang, and Selangor, the Semai are the most numerous at almost 18,000, followed by the Temiar (over 12,000). Other smaller groups, distinct from the Senoi, are the creative Mah Meri of coastal Selangor, the Jah Hut of Pahang, who are also excellent wood-carvers, and the shy Che' Wong of Pahang's deep forests who number only around 200.

Differentiated by their Malay dialects, the Orang Asli of Melaka, Negeri Sembilan, and southern Johor are also known as Proto-Malays and probably have the same distant ancestral roots as the Malays. Of these, the Jakun and the Temuan are the most numerous, each with populations of over 9,000. Although their lifestyle is similar to that of the Senoi, they have always had more contact with the Malays and Chinese, since much of their income derived from the collection of rainforest products like rattans, resins, and jungle latex. Their intimate knowledge of these valued international commodities was remarked upon even in the early days of the Melakan sultanate, when they were known as *hamba Melayu*, 'subjects of the Malays'. These days, they still have this market cornered.

Other Orang Asli groups, like the Orang Kanak from Johor's west coast which number only 40, and the more numerous Orang Seletar from the Straits of Johor, are the descendants of the Orang Laut, the 'sea people' who constituted the original navy of the Melakan sultanate and played a pivotal role in the region's history. The Laksamana, or admiral of the fleet, commanded the Orang Laut fleets which were vital for defending the sultanate, and Hang Tuah, the most famous warrior and admiral of this 'golden age', was apparently from Orang Laut roots.

Of all the Peninsular peoples, the Orang Asli are the most affected by the march of progress. Although many still live on the fringe of the forest and remain adept at hunting and gathering, the young people are becoming educated and are looking to the outside world with its wider choice of employment and opportunity. But not all are lured by the new lifestyle. The author came across the Batek while trekking in the Kenong Rimba Wilderness. They bounded along the forest paths with a tread so sure and certain, unlike ours as we stumbled over tree roots in our so-called jungle footwear. While we alien outsiders sweated profusely in the humidity and plucked leeches off our legs, the Batek were relaxed and totally in tune with their environment. I admired them for their knowledge of this great, green world, which even today most Malaysians regard with awe.

## THE MALAYS

Because of the obvious association of the Malays with Malaysia, and before that Malaya, many people are unaware that apart from being the most numerous ethnic group of this nation, the Malays are in fact one of the world's most far-flung races.

According to the 16th-century *Sejarah Melayu*, the 'Malay Annals', the original term *Melayu* was derived from the name of the river which flowed from Palembang's sacred mountain, the mystical birthplace of the rulers who went on to found Melaka. In this history, *Melayu* denotes those who were descended from this illustrious Sumatran and later Melakan lineage. In the centuries after the Melakan sultanate was forced to flee to Johor after the Portuguese invasion, the concept gradually broadened to include all those who spoke the Malay language, professed Islam and followed Malay customs. These days, the term is even more widespread and is used to describe the indigenous people of the entire Malay archipelago. It even embraces those of their ancestors who set off in their outrigger canoes eventually to populate half the globe, from Madagascar in the Indian Ocean to Hawaii.

Despite their imperial attitudes, the British colonialists liked the Malays. They admired their refined culture and their courtesy, and in their literature they stereotyped the Malay personality. 'The real Malay is courageous,' wrote Frank Swettenham, former Governor, High Commissioner and historian, in *British Malaya* (1948), 'but he is extravagant, fond of borrowing money and slow in repaying it . . . He quotes proverbs . . . never drinks intoxicants, he is rarely an opium smoker . . . He is by nature a sportsman . . . proud of his country and his people, venerates his ancient customs and traditions and has a proper respect for constituted authority . . . He is a good imitative learner . . . lazy to a degree . . . and considers time of no importance.' Swettenham was a perceptive man, and most of his generalizations had a ring of truth to them, but the tag that stuck and most annoyed the Malays was that they were lazy. The truth was that they were not inclined to work at doing something in which they were not interested. Manual labour in the tropics is not easy work and, as an early travel-writer observed, 'To sweat all day in the sun with some one else's hoe in some one else's mine merely to make money is not a pursuit which is likely to appeal to the comfortably situated Malay race.' Perhaps Swettenham should have used the word 'clever' instead of 'lazy'.

Practising the faith of Islam is inseparable from being Malay, and it is so interwoven that Muslim converts are often said to *masuk Melayu*, literally 'become Malay', when they adopt the Islamic faith. All Malaysian Malays are Muslims and it is forbidden by law to convert them to another faith. In theory, all Malay culture is governed by the code of Islam. The tenets of

*Two Malay women pose in a photographer's studio in the early 1900s.*

*A* kampung *in Johor in about 1900: its wooden houses on stilts nestle together, reflecting the close-knit lifestyle of the traditional Malay village.*

the faith are looked upon as the guidelines of Malay life. The day revolves around the five daily prayers, which to the average Malay are a natural part of their everyday routine. Yearly activities are determined by the fasting month of Ramadan, the Hari Raya celebrations at its close, and other important Islamic dates. The most important event of every Malay's life is to make the pilgrimage to Mecca. However, although Islam has been the mainstay of Malay life for over 500 years, there are remnants of early Hindu and even pagan customs that still linger in their culture, giving it a colour and variety that is uniquely Malay. To some orthodox believers these ancient customs smack of heathen practices, but for most Malays, who have already absorbed many aspects of Western life which were formerly unacceptable, they are an indispensable part of their traditional culture. Even the Arabic-style women's head-covering, which is so fashionable nowadays especially with the more religiously orthodox, was not part of Islam's original culture but was an upper-class Christian habit from the Middle East which was adopted by the Arabs.

The Malays have always been adept at accepting new ideas and incorporating them with the old. These days a BMW-driving executive, who lives in an air-conditioned apartment, still finds time to return to his ancestral *kampung* at festive times to fulfil his family obligations, and has no problems adjusting to the simple village lifestyle. Although he wears a suit and tie to the office, when he relaxes at home, returns to the *kampung*, and attends the mosque for Friday prayers, he dresses in the traditional chequered sarong and wears his characteristic brimless, fez-like cap, known as a *songkok*. He may make the odd foray to McDonald's to give the children a treat, but if given a choice he would definitely prefer the hot and tasty cuisine of his forefathers.

Except for a small minority of high-profile city businesswomen, most Malay women dress in the traditional *baju kurung*, a flattering, ankle-length suit, usually made of colourful silky fabrics, and cover their hair with a matching scarf or a short veil. At weddings and other festive occasions, the Malay knack for stylish dressing is particularly apparent. Men opt for the traditional *baju Melayu*, loose-fitting silk pants, a collarless overshirt, and a brocade cummerbund. Women wear their best silk outfits and liberally decorate themselves with pure gold jewellery.

Although western-style medicine is practised throughout Malaysia and has a huge following, the *bomoh*, a traditional medicine-man cum magician, is still an integral party of society. Many people, even highly educated Malaysians of all races, will try traditional herbal cures in lieu of surgery, or after the doctor has failed to find a cure. Although many of the chants and practices stem from animist beginnings, over the centuries Islamic prayers have been incorporated into the *bomoh*'s ritual, which is another example of the Malay's knack of blending the old with the new in order to make it acceptable. Most Malays, however sophisticated, celebrate weddings which incorporate old Hindu customs with Islamic ones, and many still believe in at least a few of the vast pantheon of ghosts and spirits which have peopled the Malaysian supernatural arena since time immemorial.

Forming around 52 per cent of Malaysia's population of 18 million, the Malays are most numerous on the Peninsula, especially in the rural areas and on the east coast, although the previously Chinese-dominated city areas now boast sizeable populations as young people educated in the villages flock to the cities for better job opportunities. As many senior family members still live in their ancestral *kampung*, at the end of Ramadan there is a huge exodus of city dwellers making the pilgrimage back to the family home; nothing beats celebrating Hari Raya in the countryside. If home is where the heart is, a Malay's soul is in the *kampung*, and even for a casual visitor to Malaysia it is not hard to understand why. For of all the memorable scenes, the traditional, wooden Malay home on stilts, shaded by tropical fruit trees and coconut palms, perhaps surrounded by rice paddies, is one of exceptional beauty. Cuthbert Woodville Harrison, who travelled to the Malay Peninsula in the 1920s, wrote that 'The Malays have given the country the only beauties in it provided by the hand of man.' The saying may today be regarded as racist, but there is more than a grain of truth in it. They are indeed a creative people, capable not only of keeping their villages picturesque, but leaders in all the arts and music, as well as the designers of South-east Asia's most celebrated contemporary architecture.

In the past, regional variations of physique, colouring, and stature denoted the various types of Malays: Kelantanese were said to be fair of skin and their women the prettiest on the Peninsula; Johoreans were the upholders of courtly traditions and spoke the finest language. Today, these generalizations are still remembered but society now has become, to use a Malay word, so much more *campur* – 'mixed-up'. Neighbours in a Kuala Lumpur street are more often than not from different states; however, just as an Englishman can differentiate between a Cockney Londoner and a Liverpudlian by listening to their speech, so can a Malaysian instantly spot a person's birthplace by the way they speak. In fact, there are some words that are only used in certain states and not in others. Natives of Penang and Kedah use the term *kupang* for ten cents, but this is not in regular usage anywhere else. Terengganu folk do not call their currency *ringgit*, but instead use the Arabic *rial*. Even the thirsty traveller sees evidence of these regional words: ice used in drinks is usually *ais*, but in Kelantan it is known as *beng*. A word may be the same, like *makan*, 'to eat', while its pronunciation varies from state to state: the 'n' is left off in Kelantan, and in Terengganu a 'g' is added, to name but two of the variations.

Ever since the Melakan sultanate, traditional rulers have played a major role in Malaysian history, and although their role today is mainly ceremonial they are still regarded by many Malays as the custodians of culture, customs and religion. In the early days they were regarded as 'god's shadow on earth', endowed with the mystical powers of *daulat*. Anyone who harmed a ruler, like the murderer of Sultan Mahmud, the last of the Melakan lineage, spent the rest of his life in agony because a wound from the dying sultan's sword sprouted grass. Even today, the murderer's descendants dare not visit Kota Tinggi where the crime took place for fear of the sultan's vengeful ghost. Traditional sultans or rajas are still the hereditary rulers of Kedah, Perlis, Perak, Selangor, Kelantan, Terengganu, Pahang, Negeri Sembilan and Johor, which gives Malaysia a large chunk of the world's surviving royal families. Regal celebrations like a royal wedding or funeral still top the television ratings, and although many Malaysians these days think the royal families should adopt less ostentatious lifestyles, and agreed in principle with the government's recent moves to limit their power, most Malays would firmly block any step to remove them, as the opposition parties have found out to their advantage.

Many different Malay groups, from all over what is now Indonesia, have been settling Malaysia for centuries, and most of the regions where they first put down roots are still bastions of their culture even today. The Minangkabau people first came from their Sumatran homeland to the Malay Peninsula during the 15th-century Melakan sultanate. Legend has it that when the Portuguese conquered Melaka, the Minangkabau fled into the interior of today's Negeri Sembilan. While all the other Malaysian cultures are patriarchal, the Minangkabau practise a unique matrilineal system known as *adat perpatih* whereby the ancestry is traced through the mother's line,

*A Melakan Malay family sit for their portrait in 1940.*

*The Sultan of Perak standing under the yellow umbrella of royalty, Kuala Kangsar, 1933.*

and the wealth and property of a family is inherited through the women's side. They believe that the original landowners of a region are the premier tribe, which leads historians to the conclusion that some of the early Minangkabau probably intermarried with the indigenous Jakun in order to secure land titles through the female side. The descendants of this prestigious first tribe still rule the state from their old royal seat of Sri Menanti. The most noticeable difference, for an outsider travelling through Negeri Sembilan, is the architecture of their houses. The roofs are curved upwards, reminiscent of a buffalo's horns – the symbol of Minangkabau culture.

Bugis, fleeing civil wars in Sulawesi, settled in Selangor from the 17th century and their influence over the history of the Malay Peninsula during this century was considerable. Francis Light, the founder of Penang, called them 'the best merchants among the eastern islands', and he considered that their patronage was the key to a port's success. They were acclaimed sailors and legendary warriors, and were often called upon by Malay chiefs to settle disputes. Gradually, though, they began taking over lands traditionally ruled by Peninsular Malays until they were the undisputed masters not only of the riverine districts of Selangor but also of Johor. The ruling families of both these states trace their roots to those early Bugis leaders.

There are also large communities of Javanese along the west coast of Johor, who keep alive traditions like the *kuda-kepang*, a trance-dance. There are other small communities like the followers of the exiled Sultan of Jambi, who fled Dutch persecution in their homeland to settle near Batu Pahat, Johor.

Although there are differences between the various Malay peoples, and their *adat*, or traditional culture, is often quite distinct, their shared language and religion were huge factors in their relatively easy assimilation into Malaysian life, unlike the immigrant Chinese, whose culture, religion and language could not be more different.

## INDIGENOUS PEOPLES OF EAST MALAYSIA

From the time the first white men came to Sarawak and Sabah, and for centuries before this, the Malays were the dominant political force, and most of this region was ruled by either the Brunei or Sulu sultanates. United by their religion and language, possessing literary skills, and being superb seamen, the Malays had a more evolved civilization than those of the inland tribes. This enabled them to play the role of overlords, even though they always were, and still remain, a minority people in East Malaysia. James Brooke, the first Rajah of Sarawak, placed Malays in authoritative positions, and they dominated the civil service, which is their preferred domain even today. Dwelling mainly along the coasts, but also found along the lowland river-banks, the Malays are happiest when they are beside the water, and as a result their homes are usually built on stilts above the low-lying ground that they favour.

The Bajau of Sabah, nicknamed the 'sea gypsies', are the most colourful of all the Malay-speaking peoples of East Malaysia. Legend has it that they owe their traditionally seaborne lifestyle to a historical event which happened around 700 years ago. A princess from Johor was betrothed to the Sultan of Sulu, but she preferred a dashing prince from Brunei. While she was being escorted to Sulu by a large contingent of Johorean war-boats, they were set upon by Bruneians, who absconded with the princess back to their homeland. The warriors were too shamefaced to return to Johor, and feared for their safety if they put into ports in either Brunei or Sulu. They were forced to lead a seafaring existence, until they gradually settled along the northern Sabah coast where they are still numerous. Some, the Bajau Laut, still prefer to live on their boats, seldom coming to land, but most live a settled existence. At Mengkabong, half an hour's drive north from Kota Kinabalu, the Bajau live a semi-waterborne life, dwelling in houses built on stilts over the water, and connected by board walks. Housewives paddle their *sampan* to visit the neighbours, and children can swim before they can walk. Further inland, at Kota Belud, a different strain of Bajau are dubbed the 'cowboys of the East', for their skills at riding and raising horses. As horses are not indigenous to Borneo, there are various, more or less fanciful, stories of their origin, the most imaginative being that they were survivors of a shipwrecked Chinese junk belonging to Kublai Khan.

In the 19th century, the Illanun, a Malay-speaking people who originated from Mindanao, were so feared by Malaysia's coastal people, even on the Peninsula, that the word for 'pirate' to this day is *lanun*. These days they live peacefully in the same areas of Sabah as the Bajau, but around the turn of the century the Bajau believed that the Illanun possessed mystical powers and could turn themselves into fish or evil spirits and even partake of a meal of human flesh. Because of this, the Bajau used to keep a close watch on those who had recently died.

Other Malay-speaking peoples of Sabah include the numerous and influential Suluk, who originated from the Sulu sultanate which once controlled northern Sabah; the amazingly agile Idahan who collect edible birds' nests from the roofs of caves; the formerly slave-trading Tidung; the Bugis; and Cocos Islanders who have immigrated here over the last century.

The Melanau, who resemble the Malays physically and in their lifestyles, are

Sarawak's original coastal inhabitants. Being in close contact with the Muslim Malays, most have now converted to Islam, though their language resembles that of the inland Kayans. Because they lived on the river-banks beside the vast peat swamps, the Melanau's traditional economy revolved around the sago palm. This plant provided them not only with their food staple and roofing material, but was also used as a valuable trade item. Like the Bajau, they are extremely amphibious and their lifestyle is intimately entwined with the water.

Coastal people have always had the most contact with outside influences, and as a result their cultures and religions have changed with the times. As a general rule, the further inland people live the less contact they have with other ethnic groups, and Sarawak's and Sabah's interior tribes are testimony to this generalization.

The Iban, Borneo's most legendary people, immortalized by their relish for headhunting, were mistakenly given the name of Sea Dayaks by Europeans who met them in sea forays, but they are actually an inland people. Sarawak's most numerous ethnic group, they originally came from the Kalimantan region of Borneo, but by the 19th century the Iban had settled throughout inland Sarawak. Although they have successfully permeated all levels of society, and many have become Christians, the Iban still have enormous reverence for their original culture and festivals, and many still live in longhouses. On the Skrang River, an Iban stronghold, the average longhouse contains around 26 separate family apartments which, contrary to the usual 'communal life' concept, are as private as any modern flat.

*A Kenyah playing a* sapeh *(lute) in the 1930s: the Kenyah people of Sarawak are renowned for their musicianship and artistry.*

The Skrang River saw heavy fighting during the early days of the 'White Rajahs', and century-old skulls, blackened with age, still hang from some longhouse centre-poles. Elders still sport tribal tattoos and are adept at storytelling and time-honoured dances. Iban youth are more interested in football and television, but longhouse life is still a reality and many traditions, including the planting of hill rice and skills in handicrafts, are still pursued.

Living almost exclusively in the south-east tip of Sarawak, the Bidayuh, formerly known as Land Dayaks, were much less war-like than the Iban, who used to pursue

these peaceful people to add to their collections of heads. Anthropologists suggest that some Bidayuh beliefs spring from Hinduism as they are the only Sarawak people who cremate their dead; also some of their pagan deities resemble those of the Hindu pantheon. Although the practice has died out these days, Bidayuh women used to cover their lower legs with brass rings, which was unique amongst Bornean people.

In the upper reaches of the Rajang and Baram Rivers live the Kayan and the Kenyah people who originally came from Kalimantan like the Iban, their traditional enemies. However, they have little else in common as they are physically larger, have paler skin, different languages, traditions, and social systems. Travellers to the upper Baram can still meet Kayan and Kenyan people who sport their distinctive stretched earlobes and wear intricately woven hats made of palm leaves. They are excellent boatmen, as any visitor to Gunung Mulu National Park will testify, and are liveliest in the evening (they are Borneo's best-known entertainers). After a few rounds of rice wine it is not unusual for a Kenyah to jump up for an impromptu 'hornbill dance', invariably encouraging the audience to join in.

Sabah's largest indigenous group, the Kadazan, always reside within sight of their sacred peak, Mount Kinabalu, which towers over most of the state's central and eastern region. As prosperous rice-farmers, the Kadazan have been in the forefront of the state's economic thrust since its earliest days, and are found in all occupations, including politics – Sabah's first Chief Minister was a Kadazan. Their traditional black outfits trimmed with silver braid are now worn only at celebrations, but their artistry with bamboo is still evident in the inland rice-growing areas like Tambunan: houses, fences, and backpacks for carrying firewood are all made with bamboo. Although many Kadazan are now Christians, age-old ceremonies centred around the rice-spirit are still enacted at the annual harvest festival.

*Iban warriors in ceremonial dress with hornbill-feather head-dresses, Kuching, in about 1900.*

Other inland agriculturists include the Kelabit from the highlands of Sarawak's Bario plateau where they grow Malaysia's highest quality rice; the Murut from the hilly border region between Sabah and Sarawak who practise shifting agriculture as well as hunting and gathering; and the Rungus, related to the Kadazan, from the Kudat region of Sabah, whose women wear distinctive black sarongs, brass bracelets, and beaded necklaces.

Although East Malaysia's only true nomads, the Penan, are the least numerous of all its indigenous peoples, international concern over the clearing of rainforests has meant that they are probably now the most renowned. Known as either Penan or Punan, the vast majority now live semi-settled lives in villages on the edge of their traditional hunting-grounds. However, some still prefer their original nomadic lifestyle in the remote rainforests of the upper Baram and Rajang river regions. Although other Bornean peoples are adept at hunting and gathering in the forest, nomadic Penan are the only group who spend their entire lives inside the rainforest. They temporarily camp near stands of wild sago which provide their food staple, but they always move on before the sago is finished to ensure that the plant will recover – just one of many sound conservation practices that the Penan utilize in all aspects of their lifestyle. From a lifetime spent in the shaded, twilight world of the forest, the Penan have the palest skins of all Bornean peoples, and many still attribute sickness in the new settlements to the malignant effect of the sun, which they traditionally feared.

In the old days the Penan were often looked upon as something like the private property of Kayan and Kenyah chiefs, as they had close trading links with these indigenous groups. Contrary to their reputation as being purists as regards conservation, the Penan were expert at gathering the prized talismans known as bezoars – concretions found in the gut of leaf-eating monkeys – the dried bladders of Honey Bears and rhinoceros horn which they traded with the Kayan and Kenyah, who in turn bartered this forest produce with Chinese traders on the coast.

Finding a solution to the Penan problem is far from easy. With the rainforests being rampantly logged, their traditional nomadic life is also endangered, as are some of the lifestyles of neighbouring indigenous peoples who still depend on the rivers and the forest to supplement their food crops. History shows that nomadic people usually settle down, but what of those who happen to prefer their original lifestyle? The Malaysian government is re-evaluating its policies and seems to be heading in the right direction of preservation rather than destruction. Ironically, it is the nation's oldest inhabitants whose ideas on sustainable land use are the most up-to-date. As Lord Shackleton wrote in his afterword for *Mulu – The Rainforest* in 1980: 'Conservation actually makes sound economic sense, as people like the Penan, who have come to terms with their environment, already know full well.'

## LATER ARRIVALS – THE CHINESE, INDIANS, AND OTHER MINORITIES

As Malaysia straddles the dominant maritime trade route to the Far East, small communities of Chinese, Indians and other foreigners had existed in most trading centres since ancient times. Chinese contacts with both Peninsular and East Malaysia date back a millennium, and the Indian connection was made even earlier, with conservative estimates of the first arrivals placed at around 1,700 years ago. If Malaysian demographics had not been so radically altered during the British colonial era, these races would still be very small minorities, as are the Arabs who, in common with the Chinese and Indians of past centuries, ostensibly came to trade. However, the British Empire was most interested in seeing Malaysia's economy boom: in order to extract the vast amounts of tin, and tap the miles of rubber trees needed to keep the coffers full, thousands of workers were needed and obtained. It was not difficult to recruit Chinese, for they were only too pleased to escape the cycle of poverty into which they had been born. Lured by the 'rags to riches' tales of migrants who had made their fortunes, the *sinkeh*, or 'new visitors', who were bound to their employers by a credit ticket system, flocked to the Nanyang, 'The Southern Ocean'. Nineteenth-century figures record the spectacular explosion of the Chinese population in Malaysia; community numbers in the 1830s rarely exceeded 500, but in 1870 there were 10,000 miners in Sungai Ujung alone. Kuching, which was a Malay village in 1840, was a Chinese town by the end of the century.

Conditions for the immigrants were nothing short of appalling. Disease, back-breaking toil, the unfamiliar climate, all took their toll and the mortality rate in some areas reached 50 per cent. But there were just as many who persevered and survived against the odds, even making their fortunes. The British were well aware of the benefits of having a large Chinese population: taxes levied on opium, pawnbroking and pork guaranteed a large revenue.

Teochew and Cantonese came from Guangdong, the Hokkien from Fukien, the Hakka from the mountainous southern regions, and the Hainanese from their island home. They brought not only their own religion, culture and differing dialects, but their own co-operative societies which formed the basis of their economic success. Even these days, the different language groups still dominate certain trades and often favour their own ethnic clan in business affairs, language being the biggest divider of the Chinese. A 1980s survey of Melaka's businesses shows patterns that are typical of any large Malaysian town. Hakkas are the goldsmiths, pawnbrokers, and owners of textile and clothing shops; the Hokkiens and Teochews control sundry goods, rice, sugar, and rubber; the Hainanese are coffee-shop proprietors (most famous for their *kai fan* or 'chicken-rice'); the Henghuas, a sub-group of the Hokkiens, dominate in electrical goods, bicycle, motorbike, and car businesses; and the Cantonese control the photography shops. Today, the Chinese constitute around a third of the Peninsular population, about 30 per cent of Sarawak's total, and 20 per cent of Sabah's. A cursory glance, however, at shop-fronts or business registers in every Malaysian city or town, is proof of their commercial dominance on both sides of the South China Sea.

Most of Malaysia's Chinese are the descendants of the 19th-century immigrants, and although they have been in Malaysia for generations, they have preserved their languages and culture intact. So much so, in fact, that in some urban centres a traveller would be forgiven for thinking, as Henri Fauconnier did on his first arrival, that he 'had landed in a Chinese city'. Every city and town has its Chinatown, even in the predominantly Malay states of Kelantan and Terengganu. In these ethnic ghettos, the streets are lined with southern-Chinese-style shophouses adorned with calligraphy, where thriving family businesses sell sharks' fins, birds' nests, and medicines – some still made from endangered species. In the incense-shrouded interiors of the bustling temples, fashionably dressed professionals and housewives alike burn joss-sticks in order to appease the gods of prosperity and good luck, just as their forefathers did.

If the Chinese of migrant descent are accused of failing to 'Malaysianize' – many still speak very little Malay after generations of habitation here – the minority group known variously as the Babas, the Straits Chinese, or the Peranakan are considered to be models of cultural integration. Originally of trader stock, their ancestors settled in Melaka as far back as the 15th century. The Babas also claim to have royal roots, as when Sultan Mansur Shah married the Chinese princess Hang Lih Po in 1459 her entourage of 'five hundred youths of noble blood' apparently settled at the foot of Bukit Cina (Chinese Hill). Obviously, some would have married local women, as did many merchants in later centuries, for during the Ch'ing Dynasty, from the 17th to the early 20th century, Chinese women were prohibited from emigrating.

Although they consistently practised their own religions, the Babas, as the menfolk are known, and the Nonyas, their women, adopted Malay customs and dress and spoke their own Malay dialect. Their own unique cuisine uses the same ingredients as Malay cooking, but they had their personalized porcelain sent from China. By the 1970s, this minority group was almost an endangered species, but these days the Babas are experiencing a revival. In Melaka, their heartland, old women with their hair in chignons, wearing the traditional batik sarong and embroidered jacket, can still be seen in the streets of old Chinatown, especially Jalan Tun Tan Cheng Lock. Their cavernous ancestral homes, decorated with plaster reliefs, tiled foyers and carved doors, still dominate this street, named after the famous millionaire Baba who was a leading engineer of independence.

The Babas enjoyed a 'Golden Age' during British rule, when many made their fortunes running rubber and gambier plantations. Obviously, their knack of harmonizing with the Malays, their long acceptance of Malaya and not China as their homeland, and their loosening of traditional Chinese social bonds, made them easily accepting of new values which the Dutch and, later, the British imposed, and this was the key to their success. Like other businessmen worldwide, the Great Depression severely eroded the Babas' fortunes. Families were forced to sell off antique furniture and priceless heirlooms just to survive, which ironically started off the Melakan antique business. However, some famous families are still wealthy, and the Babas can be found today in government service, teaching, law, architecture and management.

Indians first arrived in the Malay Peninsula as merchants trading in the textiles of Gujerat, Coromandel, Malabar and Bengal, which became important items in the Malay economy. This is evidenced even today by the immense popularity of Indian-made men's sarongs, known as *pelekat*, which originated from the Indian port of the same name. Gujerati traders were the most prominent, and in Melaka's heyday they accounted for a quarter of the estimated 4,000 merchants who lived in the city. The name *Keling* (pronounced 'kling'), for Tamil traders from the Coromandel coast, was not formerly derogatory, but these days it is considered in bad taste, although many villagers still use it in the old way. Melaka's Kampung Keling ('the Kling's village'), with its historic mosque, is where many of the wealthy trading families lived, and even in the 15th-century Melakan sultanate, Indians were prominent in society. In some cases, like Raja Kasim's Tamil uncle, they even married into royalty. When the Portuguese invaded Melaka, the Muslim Indians urged the sultan to make a *jihad* (a religious war) against them. They fully understood their power, having seen much of Indian trade fall into Portuguese hands. When the infidel Europeans took control of the city the Muslim Indians left for other ports. The Hindu Tamils, however, supported the Portuguese and became the richest merchants of Melaka. They were 'very corpulent with big bellies' according to the 16th-century historian, Duarte Barbosa. When the Dutch took control, however, the Hindus were castigated as Portuguese collaborators, and many sold their businesses to Muslim merchants. By the time the British took over the Indians had lost control of the spice trade and with it their wealth. Of the earliest Indian communities only the small minority known as the Melaka Chitties survive. Like the Baba Chinese they have adopted many Malay customs over the years, including Malay language, food, and dress.

In common with the early Chinese communities, the Indian groups were primarily based in port towns. Their numbers were small compared to the Malays, until the great migrations began under British rule. These saw the size of the Indian community explode from a few thousand to the present ten per cent of Peninsular Malaysia's population. At first Tamil labourers from South India were brought in under indentures to build roads and railways, or work on plantations. This proved unpopular, however, and was replaced by the *kangani* system: overseers in India recruited workers who came freely to work in Malaya, where they ensured the success of the rubber industry. However, compared to the urban Indian merchants and moneylenders, the estate workers rarely ventured far from the plantations. Although many of their descendants have now successfully ventured into all walks of Malaysian life, a large percentage still remains a depressed minority unable to break away from life on the estates. Like Indians the world over, Malaysia's community proudly keep up their traditional customs and religions, and speak their own dialects.

Well-known for their musical ability, the Portuguese Eurasians are probably the nation's most fascinating ethnic minority. They are the direct descendants of Melaka's Portuguese conquerors who ruled the town from 1511 until the Dutch took over in 1641. They are living testimony to a remark made by Joao de Barros, a 16th-century Portuguese traveller, that the boundary marks of the empire were material things that time could destroy, 'but it will not destroy the religion, customs and language which the Portuguese have left in those lands'. Although the Portuguese departed over 350 years ago, the descendants of those who originally intermarried with local folk still live in Melaka's Portuguese Settlement. Some of the old people speak Cristao, an archaic Portuguese which has been passed down through the generations, as have traditional dances, an Iberian-style cuisine – albeit Malaysianized – and their enduring Roman Catholic faith.

## CULTURE AND BELIEFS

### EARLY PAGAN BELIEFS

'Tradition comes down from the mountains,' according to an old Malay saying, 'but religion comes from the sea.' In so few words, this adage sums up the history of Malaysian beliefs: all the pagan practices evolved from the interior, while all the great faiths – Hinduism, Buddhism, Islam and Christianity – were brought by sea-borne missionaries.

In the beginning, everything contained its own spirit, or *semangat* – which loosely translated means 'the soul', or 'the spirit of life'. Inhabiting rocks, mountains, trees, rivers, lakes and seas, these spirits had to be appeased as it was believed that they had power over all natural forces. Most indigenous groups had shamans who acted as the intermediaries between the people and the spirit world. The Jakun's shaman was said to have the ability to turn into a tiger at whim, a phenomenon that some historians believe originated from before the Proto-Malays left their original South Chinese birthplace, as this magical ability is thought to have been learnt from the Mongols before they settled in Tibet. The Iban used to suspend the body of a dead shaman from a tree, just as the Mongolians always elevated the bodies of deceased magicians.

These days, Selangor's Mah Meri carve their spirit sculptures mainly for collectors of primitive art, but a few are still used for their original purpose in assisting the *bomoh* to rid a patient's body of sickness. First, the tranced magician would contact the spirits for advice on what image to use, then he would instruct the carver to make the sculpture. After presenting offerings of eggs, rice, and sometimes a chicken, the *bomoh* would call on the spirit to help him cure the patient. After the ritual, the carved image was thrown away, or hung from a tall tree, as the Mah Meri believe that after it had removed the sickness it was contaminated. This is the main reason why so few old carvings remain in existence.

Many Malay beliefs originate from early pre-Islamic times, predating even those traditions which were brought by early Hindus. Although not so widespread now, practices thought to bring good fortune are still followed, such as the use of a tiny reaping knife to cut rice in order not to frighten its soul, the renaming of an ill child in order to change its luck, the formal offering of betel-nut before a betrothal, and the practice amongst women when sowing rice of letting their hair hang loose to ensure a luxuriant crop.

As a person's *semangat* dwelt not only in their spit, sweat, hair, and nail-clippings, but also in their shadow, the water in which they washed their body, and their names, any of these could be used against that person through sorcery. The practice of calling children by names other than their own is still prevalent in Malay society. Nicknames are commonplace, and titles like 'the oldest aunty' or 'the youngest uncle' are in everyday use. There are still cases of the unscrupulous obtaining nail-clippings in order to put a spell on their owner, or a lovesick suitor approaching a *bomoh* in order to steal the spirit of a girl who will not return his affection.

Despite the complete acceptance of Western medicine, many Malaysians still visit the *bomoh* with mysterious illnesses that it has failed to remedy, or even in order to avert an operation that has been said by a doctor to be the only cure. Although there are sceptics, few will deny that traditional medicine often works and even effects miraculous cures. The *bomoh* usually learns his art from a master who passes on the secret incantations needed to cure sickness, though some claim to inherit the gift through miraculous means. They believe that illnesses are often caused by the patient's behaviour, and that in many cases an evil spirit has entered the body and taken over the person's soul. The incantations contain ancient verses from pantheist times, but many now include Koranic phrases, and all magicians begin by invoking Allah and end with the name of Muhammad, the Holy Prophet. In this way, a *bomoh* ensures that God is helping him.

In rural villages, the local magician is still a popular figure. Children who cry all the time, or who have no energy, are often brought along for his advice and expertise. Herbal remedies, obtained locally from the forest, are often more effective and cheaper than those prescribed by a doctor. Fish-bones caught in the throat, skin complaints, problems with virility, menstruation and broken bones are conditions that are commonly treated by a *bomoh* with excellent results.

Some royal courts still keep a *pawang*, a magician versed in the secret arts to safeguard the royal lineage, who also recites incantations to keep the rain away during important functions. Those skilled in the collection of *gaharu*, a scented wood, and *kapur*, camphor, and in the catching of crocodiles and elephants, are also known as *pawang*. Loosely translated, the name means 'one who combines magic and skill in his profession'.

All Malays close their windows at sunset, the time of the evening prayer, but even before Islam arrived this part of the day was considered dangerous: it was the time when the yellow spirits of the west – the region of the dead – were abroad. Lonely forest haunts were also peopled with a vast pantheon of spirits, some of which not only still bring fear into the hearts of rural Malays, but are also well-known to their Chinese and Indian neighbours. Often a person's sickness will be attributed to their going into the forest, returning never to be the same again. A *pontianak*, an evil spirit that preys on women in childbirth, was even said to have been spied recently beside a popular restaurant in Melaka's Portuguese Settlement. *Hantu*, or ghosts, are still sighted not only by incredulous rural folk, but by city dwellers of every degree of sophistication.

In order to placate the earth spirits, offerings are usually made. Chickens are ritually slaughtered once a year on the slopes of Mount Kinabalu by the Kadazan who make their living as guides and porters on Malaysia's highest peak. Early accounts claim that the Iban used to crush a slave girl under the main pillar of a new longhouse, a sacrifice for which a chicken is now substituted.

Only a generation ago the Malays still followed a considerable ritual in their house-building, and in some remote villages certain aspects of this tradition are still adhered to, being considered essential for the well-being of the inhabitants. The placing of the centre-pole, known as a *tiang seri*, was most important as it was here that the house spirit dwelt. Incense was first burnt at the chosen site, then after measuring a length of rattan and a stick to the length of her outstretched arms, the housewife gave these to the *bomoh*, who tied the rattan to the stick and planted it at the house site together with a brimming bucket of water. The following day the stick and the string were measured. If they had shrunk the site was considered inauspicious, but if they had grown it was deemed suitable. Similarly, if the water had overflowed it was a good omen but a fall in its level was a bad sign. If one test was positive then the location was approved and it was here that the central column was placed. When the column was raised, the household held a feast for the village, prayers from the Koran were read, and rice-flour, believed to frustrate evil, was sprinkled on the column. Pieces of white, black, and red cloth, symbolizing the mysterious unseen forces – namely life, courage and purity respectively – were placed on top of the column to keep away malicious spirits, and coins were placed underneath to ensure a prosperous future for the inhabitants and to help them appease the house spirit.

Even the Chinese have taken some original pantheist concepts into their religious practices. Huge Tualang trees are often left standing because they are believed to be the dwelling-places of spirits. Some have had altars built beside them where devotees present offerings to the resident deity. Graveyards and haunted houses are often visited by avid gamblers with a belief in the supernatural who are credited with obtaining 'lucky numbers' from the resident spirits.

## HINDUISM ARRIVES

With the coming of Hinduism, possibly around the beginning of the first millennium AD, Malay culture underwent its first major upheaval. There are few tangible clues that Hinduism, and also Buddhism, which arrived around the fourth century, ever existed, probably because, as the *Kedah Annals* relate, when the Malays converted to Islam they destroyed all their idols. However, a wealth of cultural traditions obviously had their beginnings in these early contacts with Indian civilization. Sanskrit words in the Malay language show that astronomy, textile-dyeing, the potter's wheel, glass, monumental architecture, and irrigated rice cultivation were all imports from India. However, the most influential of all these was Hindu philosophy and the concept of a godlike ruler.

One of the most elaborate rituals to be passed down from the Hindu era, and which still survives today, is the enthronement ceremony of a Malay ruler, in which he acquires a quasi-divine status. First he is bathed to wash away his old presence, then, wearing necklets and armlets, he has a 'lightning' seal thrust into his head-dress – a gesture reminiscent of Vedic practice. Indra, the Hindu god of weather, who controlled lightning and rain, was thought to be a ruler in earthly form. It is probably no coincidence that the early capital of Pahang was called Indrapura – 'the town of Indra' – and that the name of the hill behind the royal palace at Sri Menanti in Negeri Sembilan translates as 'the hill of Sri Indra'. In early Malay literature dynastic genealogies mention that the kings of mythical Kalinga (in India) were among their ancestors.

Another ceremony which has its roots in Hindu traditions, and is currently under threat from orthodox Muslims, is that which precedes the performance of a shadow puppet play based on the *Ramayana*. The puppet-master, taking on the guise of Vishnu, gives offerings to the spirits of heaven and earth, and to Siva as Nataraja, lord of dancers and king of actors. He waves his leather puppets through incense smoke to drive away the evil spirits. (See page 47.)

In everyday life, the Malay marriage ceremony known as the *bersanding* is one of the most evident traditions to have survived since Hindu times. The solemn countenance of the bride and groom, the sitting in state when they are dressed as 'rajas for a day', and their ritual feeding each other with rice are all remnants of Indian culture. More devout Muslims sometimes forego the *bersanding* part of the marriage ceremony as everyone is more or less aware of its Hindu origins, but for most Malays, this is all part and parcel of their rich cultural heritage and is an integral element of every wedding.

Other life events are also marked by traditions from these times, like the ceremony known as *melenggang perut*, 'rocking the stomach', which is done in the seventh month of pregnancy; the whispering of a baby's name into its ear; and the shaving of a boy's head except for a lock of hair which is cut at puberty (though the last-mentioned practice has just about died out these days).

Hinduism also lives on in its original form, as it is the major religion of Malaysia's Indians who constitute around ten per cent of the population. Deepavali, the Hindu festival of lights, is a public holiday in Peninsular Malaysia, and many other traditional festivals are celebrated throughout the year. Perhaps the most spectacular of all these is Thaipusam, held in late January or early February to celebrate Subramaniam's victory over evil forces. Penitents shoulder massive *kavadis* and pierce their flesh with skewers to gain favour with the gods. In Kuala Lumpur, the tranced participants climb 272 stairs up a limestone cliff-face to a sacred shrine deep in the caverns of Batu Caves. It is not unusual for crowds of up to 800,000 to turn out for Malaysia's most ostentatious show of devotion. Onlookers often wonder why the participants are willing to put up with so much pain, but after removing his metre-long skewers from his tongue, a Tamil office clerk denies there is any pain attached, as by putting himself into a tranced state he has elevated his mind from the physical to the spiritual realm.

## ISLAM – THE NATIONAL FAITH

Islam was the most successful of all the great faiths to enter South-east Asia, establishing itself throughout the Malay Archipelago. The faith of Muhammad did not reach South-east Asia on the blade of a sword: a peaceful conversion was initiated by wealthy Arab and Indian traders. Psychologically it had great attractions, for its revolutionary concepts freed its adherents from the feudal bondage of Hinduism. In Islam all men are equal – the pauper can kneel beside the sultan to pray – and this equalizing force probably represented the greatest single democratic change in the region's history. By the 14th century Islam had permeated both sides of the Melaka Straits and the South China Sea. Ibn

*The Masjid Jamek in Kuala Lumpur, built in 1909 at the confluence of the city's two rivers, the Gombak and the Kelang. These days it is dwarfed by KL's modern high-rise buildings.*

Batutah, the celebrated Arab traveller who visited Sumatra in 1323, wrote of its rich trading kingdoms and of its Muslim ruler who was 'a humble-hearted man who walks on foot to the Friday prayer'. This was a far cry from the Hindu raja who was usually carried abroad, never letting his feet touch the earth. From Sumatra, Islam moved across to Malaysia where the sultans embraced the faith with a fervour that is still as apparent today, 600 years later.

From the dawn call of the muezzin, as punctual as the cock's crow, to the sonorous *Allah hu-Akbar* – 'God is Great' – of the evening prayer, Islam pervades all of Malay life. Enter a mosque, be it a simple wooden construction or the vast domed National Mosque in Kuala Lumpur, and inside there is a simplicity which distinguishes itself from the other great faiths. There are no icons, no pews, no altars, but a great open space where the faithful lay their prayer mats on the floor and give thanks to Allah facing in the direction of Mecca, the holy centre of Islam. Islam seems eminently suitable for the tropics, with its emphasis on water for cleansing the body and its open-sided structures for prayers. Its great festival times are not the colourful celebrations of Malaysia's other religions, but they are centred on the family – feasts to end the fasting month, or for the culmination of the Haj, the pilgrimage to Mecca.

Everyday life for a Malay revolves around Islam and its five principles: namely, the acceptance of the *kalimah shahadah*, that there is no god but Allah and that Muhammad is his messenger; the five daily prayers; the month-long fast of Ramadan; the payment of *zakat* (a charitable tax for the poor); and an undertaking to make the Haj (if one is financially able) once in a lifetime. For a non-Muslim, some of these tenets, like the daily prayers, may seem excessive, but to the average Malay taking time out to pray is an everyday part of existence which fits neatly into their way of life. Various prayer times are used as a way to divide up the day. Just as people of other cultures may talk about going out after sunset, the Malay will call it 'after the evening prayer'; similarly, 'before dawn' would be described as 'before the morning prayer'. However, the Malay day starts at the previous sunset, so a 'Sunday market', for instance, will be held on Saturday night, often confusing the unknowing visitor who turns up on the Sunday morning to find the market-place deserted.

For a Muslim, the most joyous time of the year is the fasting month, known either as Ramadan (its Arabic title), or as *puasa*, which simply means 'fasting'. From the first light of dawn until the setting of the sun not a drop of water nor a crumb of food will pass the lips of most Malays. Cigarette smoking, sexual relations, and aggressive talk are also refrained from during these hours as the idea of fasting is to cleanse not only the body but also the spirit. Ironically, though, for a connoisseur of Malay cuisine Ramadan is the best month of the year, for this is the time when housewives make all kinds of delicacies (many only seen during this festive month) and sell them at street markets for the daily breaking of the fast. Economically it also makes sense, for this is how many women make extra money to buy the family the new outfits they will wear at the festival time of Hari Raya, which starts the morning after the new moon is sighted. Houses are washed, cakes and biscuits are made days in advance, new curtains are hung, all for the month-long 'open-house' which is not only an integral part of the Malays' religion, but is part of their inherited tradition known as *adat*.

*Biar mati anak, jangan mati adat*, which means 'lose a child rather than a custom', is an old Malay proverb which is evidence of the importance that traditional culture plays in everyday life. Some orthodox Muslims point out that much of this *adat* has its beginnings in pre-Islamic times, but as these influences have also become entwined with Muslim practices, like the celebration of Hari Raya, or a boy's circumcision, it is difficult to separate the wheat from the chaff. Because the origins of many practices have now been forgotten, most Malays rightly believe that their lives would be less meaningful and their culture would suffer if everything that was judged as pre-Islamic was thrown out simply because it evolved from an earlier era. For what are people without their culture?

## OTHER FAITHS

Malaysia's most colourful, noisy, and visually exciting celebrations must be the various festivals of its Chinese community. At Chinese New Year, youths dressed as huge lions cavort to the sounds of raucous cymbal bands, and until very recently, when they were banned, the evening that ushered in the start of the New Year was a cacophony of fireworks. At Yulan, the Festival of the Hungry Ghosts, when the souls of the dead roam the earth, bonfires of sacred joss-papers are burnt and street operas known as *wayang* are staged.

In the 1940s, when an official census on religion was organized, the secretary of a Buddhist association declared that Malaya's Chinese Buddhists were either 'burning Buddhists . . . [who] spend a lot of money and time setting fire to candles, joss sticks, and the models of houses and goodness knows what, and they are not too clear what they are doing it for', or they were 'non-burning Buddhists', like the members of the secretary's own association, who were against these practices believing that they had nothing to do with real Buddhism. Today, the picture is still very much the same, and as well as 'burning Buddhists' there are millions of Chinese who practise their ancestor religions like Taoism and Confucianism with just as much emphasis on the burning of joss-sticks and joss-papers.

Enter most Chinese temples and this practice is immediately apparent. The air is thick with incense smoke, especially near the altars, where each devotee waves handfuls of joss-sticks in obeisance to the gods. Huge brass urns filled with sand prickle with hundreds of sticks, and when they are spent the temple assistant takes them out to an incinerator, usually to the side of the temple, where they are burnt together with the sacred joss-papers. At the 17th-century Cheng Hoon Teng in Melaka, Malaysia's oldest Chinese house of worship, the huge roof beams are a glossy black, stained from centuries of incense smoke. At this temple, typical of many across the country, adherents of all the Chinese faiths come to pray at the various altars. Pride of place belongs to Kwan Yin, however. She is the Goddess of Mercy, and is a favourite deity amongst the Malaysian Chinese. Her bronze image, imported from India in the 19th century, bears more than a passing resemblance to Queen Victoria who coincidentally ruled the empire at that time. At another lesser altar, devotions are made to Kwan Ti. Originally the God of War, he is now more often associated with prosperity and wealth, and is a popular recipient of the prayers of many businessmen and women. Most of the reasons behind the rituals of China's ancestor religions have been lost in the mists of time, and now it is difficult to ascertain whether they are solely religious traditions and practices or a reflection of moral and social codes. However, most of Malaysia's Chinese would take no interest in the result of this academic dilemma, preferring to keep up their ancestral ways without question. For them they are an integral part of maintaining their ancient culture.

Other Malaysian religions include Sikhism, whose original adherents were brought out from India by the British to form their colonial police force. The Sikhs are mainly centred in the Peninsular states of Perak, Penang, and Selangor and their population stands at around 50,000. Their temples are called *gurdwara* and serve both as a centre of worship and a social centre for the community.

Around seven per cent of Malaysians are Christians and this number encompasses most of the different sects of the religion. Roman Catholicism was brought by the Portuguese who actively sought to convert the local population. However, it never found favour with the Malays, and as a result a large percentage of its followers today are the descendants of those early Portuguese. The Dutch introduced Protestantism, but they were more interested in trade than conversions and had a much more open attitude to religion. During their rule in Melaka, many of the city's still-surviving 17th-century churches, temples, and mosques were built. Missionaries were most active in Sarawak and Sabah, and converted a number of the indigenous people to the Christian faith. The Peninsula is home to a small group of Chinese whose ancestors were Protestants even before they left their homeland; other Chinese have recently been attracted by American-style charismatic sects. As Malaysia recognizes its multicultural heritage, Christmas Day is a public holiday, while Easter is a state holiday in Sarawak.

In these days when communalism is again raising its ugly head in nations as far flung as India, Bosnia, and Germany, Malaysia, with its multitude of different peoples and cultures, appears to have buried its past troubles associated with race and religion. It is now a harmonious model of cultural integration for the rest of the world.

## CULTURAL TRADITIONS

### LITERATURE

Pak Hamzah is one of a dying breed. As Malaysia's most famous and travelled shadow puppet-master, he knows that his craft is a vanishing one. These days, to be a *dalang*, as he is called, requires more time and effort than the young are prepared to give. Not only is he adept at playing all the musical instruments in the accompanying band, and making all his leather puppets by hand, he is also familiar with every facet of the 2,000-year-old *Ramayana* on which most of his performances are based. In addition, he is the sole manipulator of up to 100 puppets, relying on his prodigious memory for their differing voices, and the dialogue, narration, and songs which constitute a three-hour performance. Apart from his superb theatrical, musical, and artistic skills, Pak Hamzah is one of the last of the traditional Malay story-tellers. They were once a familiar sight entertaining villagers in the rural districts. Although many people knew how to read and write verses from the Koran, literacy was limited, and books were a rare sight, so the travelling story-teller who had a talent to entertain was a popular figure before the days of radio. His tales were sometimes adaptations from the Hindu classics, the *Mahabharata* and the *Ramayana* (known to Malays as *Hikayat Sri Rama*). Others were fairy tales, known as *hikayat*, which often featured the amazing adventures of a prince in search of fame and fortune. Sometimes they took the form of fables, and often used the tiny mouse-deer as the hero, outwitting larger creatures like crocodiles and tigers.

Although the Hindu classics became well-known to Malay audiences, nothing tangible remains of this literature in the form of Indian scripts, although the Malay language contains many words of Sanskrit origin which express religious, ethical, and social ideas, such as 'soul', 'time', 'religion', 'property', and 'fasting'. When Islam arrived, along with the Arabic script, it revolutionized the Malay language. Royal courts became centres of learning where literature became the way to record the genealogies of kings and historical events. The most famous text from this period is the *Sejarah Melayu*, 'The Malay Annals', a history of the Melakan sultanate written in the 15th or 16th century. Generally agreed to be the finest literary work in Malay, this superbly written text gives a fascinating insight into Melaka's glorious heyday. This is no dry history: personalities are faithfully portrayed and events are powerfully narrated. However, as C. C. Brown, the translator, writes: 'These vignettes owe not a little of their brilliance to the language in which the author is writing. Of Malay it has been said "As a tongue which is capable of expressing, with admirable terseness, the most minute shades of difference between every physical action, and between many states of feeling . . . Malay has probably few rivals"'.

Other famous Malay writings include the *Misa Melayu*, an 18th-century account of Perak; the *Kedah Annals* which combined earlier Hindu epics with Kedah history; and the works of Raja Ali Haji which included the *Tuhfat al-Nafis*, 'The Precious Gift', a history of the Johor empire.

When the British settled in Malaysia they brought with them new forms of literature like novels, short stories and poetry and this changed the face of the Malay literary scene. Munshi Abdullah, the official scribe to Singapore's founder, Sir Stamford Raffles, was the first Malay writer to depart from legends and myths and record contemporary events: he wrote an autobiography, *Hikayat Abdullah*, and accounts of his travels. However, although the British lauded him, and his works provide a fascinating insight into the early 19th century, he was not popular with the Malays as he often praised English values and condemned the native culture. Other writers, working later in the British period, used their pens to press for independence and voice their concern over social ills. They were a major force in making their fellow countrymen aware of their rights. After independence, and especially since the implementation of the National Language Policy which became law in 1967, Malay literature is again in the ascendant and novelists and poets, writing exclusively in their own language, are enjoying unprecedented popularity.

### MUSIC AND DANCE

Of all the Malay cultural expressions, music is the most popular. Music shows are an almost nightly event on television, and Malay singers dominate the airwaves and the hit parades. Modern musical genres span the gamut from *rentak asli*, loosely translated as 'Malay beat' which is founded in traditional musical style, to overseas-influenced heavy-metal and country and western bands.

Johor has its *ghazal*, a type of folk-singing which originated in the Middle East. In a haunting, lilting style reminiscent of Arabic melodies, the singer vocalizes popular love poems or riddles, known as *pantun*, to a musical accompaniment which includes a six-stringed Arabian lute, Indian tabla drums, violin, accordion and guitar. Melaka's *dondang sayang* are lullabies and love songs which also use the *pantun* for inspiration. Penang has its *boria*, a minstrel band which originally went serenading during Muharram, the first month of the Islamic year. And Kelantan has the *berdikir bharat*, which comprises two teams of singers who make up their rap-like repartee as they go along, accompanied by hypnotic drum beats. Also popular in Kelantan are contests between drummers playing the *rebana ubi*, a large drum made from a hollowed-out log. Points are awarded for timing, rhythm, tone, and style, and these giant drum contests have become so popular that an international event is staged every year.

The most elaborate music and dance traditions evolved in the royal courts, where music was an integral part of all ceremonial events. In downtown Alor Setar, the capital of Kedah, there is an unusual tower called the Balai Nobat which houses the sacred instruments of the royal orchestra known as the *nobat*. The three drums, a gong and a flute, were presented to the Sultan of Kedah by Melaka's Sultan Mahmud Shah in the 15th century and are still used for inaugurations, weddings and funerals. Kelantan's *mak yong*, a dance-drama performed mainly by women, was an exclusive palace entertainment for at least three centuries and is still performed during the Sultan of Kelantan's birthday celebrations. Tales of court intrigues and royal romances are popular themes, and performances often last for up to five evenings. Musicians playing gongs, drums, and a Malay viol known as a *rebab* accompany the singers. The performance is combined with special ceremonial rituals by the resident shaman to make sure everything proceeds smoothly. Traditional dances were also favoured court entertainments, like the popular *joget*. This is usually to the accompaniment of a *gamelan* band, which utilizes only percussion instruments including gongs, xylophones and drums.

Music and dance are also popular forms of entertainment amongst Malaysia's indigenous people. The Orang Asli create their music with flutes and stamping tubes of bamboo, and make mouth organs from gourds. Sarawak's Kenyah are renowned for their singing, especially when a soloist is joined in the chorus by the entire longhouse singing in harmony. Their close neighbours, the Kayan, are Borneo's best dancers. Most probably they are the originators of the hornbill dance and other 'war-dances' which were also adopted by the Iban.

## ARTS AND CRAFTS

In the old days Malay artisans and craftsmen were an integral part of the royal court: many lived and worked in the villages which grew up beside the palace. Sultans, chiefs, nobles, and their wives and families were the moneyed class, and silversmiths and goldsmiths, silk-weavers, and woodcarvers depended on royal patronage for their existence. A royal wedding was the ultimate event and every artisan was involved in preparing the trousseau and the ceremonial items needed for such a prestigious affair. However, when the courts became more westernized, rulers started buying imported jewellery, clothing, and artefacts. The habit of betel-nut chewing went out of fashion, thus rendering obsolete all the silver items which had formerly been used in its preparation and forcing many artisans to hang up their tools. Scholars in the mid 20th century predicted that many traditional arts and crafts were in danger of extinction. Fortunately, however, in the predominantly Malay-populated regions of the Peninsula's east coast, craftsmen and -women preserved their age-old practices. Today, silver working, silk-weaving, woodcarving and batik-making are all experiencing a huge revival.

Obsolete in most other states, silversmiths still thrive in Kota Bharu. They can be found hammering away on repoussé work and creating filigree jewellery in shops in Kampung Sireh, and in a government-sponsored workshop at Kampung Morak. These days, jewellery and functional pieces like fruit bowls, tea-sets and spoons are popular, and although past fashions called for different artefacts, the techniques employed and the designs used are the same. In Islam it is taboo to use anthropomorphic figures, and many of the patterns are therefore inspired by flowers, leaves, branches and even clouds. One traditional pattern is known as *awan larat*, 'continuous floating clouds'. Early silverware is often of exceptional craftsmanship and some pieces, like the earliest surviving example – a royal Johorean betel-set from the early 18th century which has a perforated design – employ a painstaking technique that is seldom seen these days. Probably the most fascinating of all the old pieces are leaf-shaped 'fig leaves' which until the 19th century were the only clothing worn by little girls.

Silk brocades, known as *kain songket*, have always been the favoured textiles for royal occasions, and these elegant woven cloths are still the preferred wear, not only for courtly occasions but for government functions. They are most often used as traditional bridal wear, when both the bride and groom are dressed in sumptuous brocade outfits. At a Kelantanese weaver's showroom, a pale mauve colour is still sold only to royalty, and there are certain designs which are even now the prerogative of the traditional ruler. Weavers are usually women who have learnt the craft from their mothers, to whom it was handed down by their mothers before them. The very best weavers would work for the palace, like the grandmother of Hajjah Ngah, the present principal weaver in Terengganu, who was picked from two thousand local artisans of her day to become the sultan's head weaver. Like most other time-honoured crafts, *songket* weaving is practised exclusively in the east coast states of Terengganu and Kelantan, and the techniques and looms used are still the same as in the old days. Woven on a simple four-posted loom, the brocade consists of a silk background with a floating weft of gold and silver threads. Designs are also passed down through generations of weavers, and a distinctive part of every length is the *kepala*, a centre panel with a particularly elaborate

*Two musicians,* c. *1905, with a nose-flute and a stringed instrument called a* busoi. *Indian, Arab, Chinese and Javanese styles have all influenced traditional Malay music.*

*Kelabit smiths in the 1920s. The bellows consisted of two hollow logs containing pistons padded with bunches of feathers which expanded and trapped the air on each downstroke, forcing it into the fire through clay pipes.*

pattern. The names of the designs echo the Malay fascination with nature and the countryside: one is known as 'bamboo shoots', another 'the tail feathers of a cock'; there are also variations on the themes like 'flowers inside the bamboo shoot'. In the old days it was a tradition for nobles to design their own *songket* patterns. This legacy lives on today as a Terengganu prince, Tunku Ismail Tunku Su, continues to create new designs at his well-known workshop.

In the 1970s, wood-carving, like many other traditional skills, was in danger of dying out, but these days patronage is on the increase. Malay wood-carvings not only adorn the walls of museums but decorate the foyers of banks, businesses, and government offices, including that of the prime minister. Some of the best wood-carving is on the panels, pillars, windows and doors of the nation's oldest royal palaces, which were all built of wood. In the old days, a wood-carver would enter the forest to select his own timber. Incantations were said to appease the forest spirits, and special mystical knowledge was needed in order to keep the wood-carver safe from tigers and other feared beasts. After selecting a suitable tree he would return with wood-cutters from his village who would fell the tree using small adzes – no mean task. Encik Long of Besut was one such master carver and during four decades of his century-long life he was the principal builder and craftsman for the Raja of Besut. Examples of his work still exist and show how upper-class houses were constructed using no nails, with beautifully carved panels which utilized not only floral patterns but superbly incised verses from the Koran.

Batik cloth is often used to symbolize Malaysia. The national airline uses it for its uniforms, batik shirts are *de rigueur* as men's formal attire and are even compulsory dress at the nation's only casino. It is also worn as sarongs and used for the fashionable women's suit known as a *baju kurung*. But batik-making is not a traditional Malay craft: it was introduced from Indonesia in the 1930s and took off only after the Second World War. However, although it is of recent origin, there is no denying that batik-making is now the nation's most popular craft. Using a wax-resist technique, the patterns are stamped on to lengths of cloth using a printing block made from zinc strips bent into the desired shapes and dipped in molten wax. However, the biggest success story is of hand-painted batiks, where the designs are drawn on the cloth using a 'wax pen' and the dyes are painted on with brushes. This latter method means that more colours can be used than with the vat-dyeing method, and the free-hand designs are limited only by the artisan's imagination. Batik workshops are now opening up all over Malaysia, but the majority of craftspeople are based on the Peninsular east coast. This area still maintains its artistic dominance, not only in silver work, silk-weaving, wood-carving, and batik-making, but in other unique crafts like ironsmithing, kite-making, and basketry.

Across the South China Sea in Sarawak and Sabah, the indigenous peoples are renowned for their skill in weaving baskets and hats. The nomadic Penan weave fine black and white baskets from split rattan. To find the best materials they often have to walk a day's journey deep into the forest, then they dry, split, and finally colour the rattan with dye made of forest leaves.

Other traditional crafts which still survive include decorated pottery from Sarawak, incised 'pumpkin pots' from Perak, gold and silver embroidery on velvet also from Perak, and baskets made from Pandanus leaves.

## TRADITIONAL ARCHITECTURE

With some of the world's oldest rainforests literally at the village door, Malay house-builders of the past certainly never lacked for adequate materials. Wood for the main structure, walls, windows and doors was obtained from the many excellent hardwood species of the nearby forest. The trunkless Nipa palm provided the thatch for the roof, and Nibong, another swamp palm, was used split into planks for the flooring. The Malays' building style was first described by a 15th-century Chinese traveller, and its basic design remains the same today. Set high on stilts to avoid floods and roaming tigers, the Malay house is still an integral and picturesque part of the rural scenery. Corrugated iron has virtually replaced thatch, and houses have evolved to suit changing tastes, such as the use of furniture, which needed higher walls. But the basic Malay house is still designed around the *rumah ibu*, literally 'the mother house', which serves as the main living area.

*A resthouse in Negeri Sembilan, with the characteristic buffalo-horn roofs of Minangkabau architecture.*

Behind this is the kitchen, and in front, the *serambi* or verandah where close friends are entertained and the family relaxes in the hot afternoons. Some houses also incorporate an *anjung*, a covered foyer where guests are greeted. In 19th-century Melaka houses this is often elaborately decorated with wood-carvings, and the front stairs are covered in Art Nouveau tiles like those at the Penghulu's House in Merlimau, Malaysia's most photographed traditional home. Melakan houses also show the influences of that state's multicultural history, such as Chinese-inspired courtyards and curved, tiled staircases.

Homes in Negeri Sembilan have distinctive roof-ridges which curve in the shape of buffalo horns, a symbol of the Minangkabau people who first settled the state. In Kelantan and Terengganu, Thai influences are apparent in the wall panelling and the gable roof ends.

In Sarawak and Sabah, the longhouse was, and in many rural areas still is, the preferred shelter. These can house two or three families, like those of the Iban, or may be as big as the huge Kayan and Kenyah longhouses where up to 40 families are lodged. Usually built on the banks of rivers, longhouses are constructed of wood, and these days most have corrugated iron roofs, though traditional roofing materials were palm thatch or ironwood shingles. The outer verandah is used for drying crops such as rice, the covered verandah is a communal area used for welcoming guests, holding feasts, and other festivities, and for weaving mats and other daily chores. In the apartments behind, each family leads its private life, and in some modern longhouses there are separate kitchens and bathrooms in this section.

## FOOD

Influenced by so many cultures, Malaysian cuisine is so renowned that some travellers come here merely to eat. And although the Chinese and Indian cuisines are equally respected it is the traditional Malay cuisine that is most representative of the country. Hot and spicy are the adjectives normally used to describe the indigenous food, which makes liberal use of chillies and spices to obtain its characteristic flavours. In the old days, and in most rural areas even today, all the ingredients were obtained locally. Coconuts, used for their milk, grew beside every house, conveniently dropping to the ground when they were ripe. Rice paddies surrounded the village, fish was caught fresh every day, fruit trees shaded each house, herbs, vegetables, tubers and yams were grown in the household plot, chickens provided eggs and meat, and at feast times a cow or a goat was slaughtered.

Most curries and other dishes are accompanied by a variety of *sambal*, which are hot, spicy sauces made by pounding chillies, garlic, *belacan* (a fermented shrimp paste), and other spices. Coconut milk, made from grated coconut which is then squeezed to extract the cream, is a basic ingredient of dishes from curries to traditional cakes, and being high in cholesterol is one of the reasons for the rich taste of Malay cuisine, and the thickening waistlines of its devotees.

*Satay* is Malaysia's best-known dish and is usually bought from roadside vendors rather than being made at home. Small cubes of marinated chicken, lamb, or beef are skewered and grilled over charcoal and then eaten with a spicy peanut sauce.

Malaysians often start the day with *nasi lemak*, rice cooked in coconut milk with side dishes such as deep-fried anchovies, peanuts, a hard-boiled egg, and salted fish. Lunch is even more elaborate as this is the main meal of the day. *Nasi campur*, literally 'mixed-up rice', is the mainstay, and at hawker stalls the customer just points to whatever curry, vegetable, meat, fish, seafood or chicken dishes he would like to accompany his rice. Noodles are equally popular and feature on all roadside menus. Known as *mee*, they can be fried with vegetables and seafood, or made into delicious soups like *laksa* which is a Penang speciality. A famous dessert is *gula melaka*, sago pudding flavoured with palm sugar and coconut milk. Fruits are plentiful and come in a marvellous variety including dozens of different types of bananas. King of the fruits is the often maligned durian, which looks like a spiky football and was described by F. Spenser Chapman as 'like eating peaches and cream whilst sitting on a lavatory'. Its repellent smell often puts off would-be eaters but if you can surmount that hurdle the taste is sublime. Other fruits which are more popular with Europeans include the hairy, red rambutan with sweet flesh like that of a lychee; the massive jackfruit – largest of all cultivated fruits – with its tangy yellow flesh; a large variety of mangoes including the delicate-tasting *kuini*; the purple-skinned mangosteen with its pinky-white, slightly acidic segments; and others like papaya, starfruit, guava, and pomelos.

## PLACES OF INTEREST

### KUALA LUMPUR – THE MOTHER CITY

When the train bearing Cuthbert Woodville Harrison, author of Malaysia's first tour guide of 1910, glided 'into Kuala Lumpur at dusk . . . a tropical sunset [was] lighting up the government offices, making them look like part of a "rose-red city half as old as time".' These buildings were then only a scant 15 years old, but their Moorish architecture featuring domes, cupolas, and archways gave the impression that they were of another more ancient age. These days, many of those 'Arabian Nights' buildings which so impressed Harrison at the beginning of the century, not only survive in South-east Asia's youngest and fastest-growing capital, but are Kuala Lumpur's trademark.

Stories of how the city was founded vary according to the tellers' cultural affiliations. The Chinese relate the tale of tin-miners heading upstream from Kelang on the Melaka Straits to found a settlement beside the junction of the Kelang and Gombak Rivers in 1857. The Malay version gives the same location except that the area was already the fief of a local chieftain. Kuala Lumpur means 'muddy estuary', a fitting name for a town that made its early fortunes with tin-mining, a pursuit which invariably muddies any stream. It was a tough old town in the early days. Chinese Triads fought their gang wars. Gambling and opium dens were the only entertainment, and the Chinese headman paid cash for the heads of his enemies. Only the fittest survived and the odds were grim. Fever carried off 70 of the 87 original prospectors in the first month. For those who made it there were riches to be made, and in a mere four decades after the town was founded Kuala Lumpur became the state capital. Thatched huts were replaced by those wonderful Moorish buildings seen today and a cosmopolitan town arose to replace the bawdy muddy estuary which Gide once called 'Kuala L'Impure'.

In the short time since the Union Jack was hauled down at independence in 1957, the city has changed beyond belief. Today's capital, with a population of at least one and a half million, is constantly expanding. Towering cranes hover above half-finished skyscrapers that create an ever-changing skyline, and new suburbs keep creeping out into the surrounding hills. Progress has not been without some losses. Kuala Lumpur's location at the head of the Kelang Valley, backed by a mountain range 1,800 metres (6,000 feet) high, is impressive, but the city's geography is similar to that of Los Angeles and brings the same problems. The valley acts as a pollution trap, especially during the windless season between monsoons. A roaring economy which enables more and more citizens to purchase their own car, an abysmal public transport service and polluting industries all contribute to the pall of smog which can often envelope the city. Fortunately, after a tropical downpour Kuala Lumpur emerges as from a chrysalis, newly bathed, with its forest-clad mountains providing a stunning backdrop.

In line with the colonial attitude of 'divide and rule', Kuala Lumpur was segregated by the Kelang River: the government administration buildings were sited on the west bank, and the commercial district, otherwise known as Chinatown, on the east bank. The hub of the city is still around the meeting of the rivers where the original settlement was made. North of here is a maze of streets and markets known as 'Little India', and east of the central business district is Kuala Lumpur's newest and richest chunk of real estate, a cluster of multinational corporations and five-star hotels, nicknamed the 'Golden Triangle' for obvious reasons.

The city's historical heart centres on Dataran Merdeka, commonly known by its colonial name, the Padang, a green swathe of lawn fronting the Tudor-style Royal Selangor Club, which survives as a remnant of colonial days. Here, the planters and colonial officials sipped their gins and tonics on the verandah overlooking the cricket field, so it was fitting that the Padang was also where independence was first proclaimed. Ringing the lawns are the famed Moorish buildings, including Malaysia's most photographed edifice, the Sultan Abdul Samad Building with its copper-domed clock tower. Further afield is the Kuala Lumpur Railway Station, which Paul Theroux called 'the grandest station in South-east Asia'. Built during the British colonial era, this edifice owes its architectural style to the state engineer of the time, who persuaded the architect to change his original Renaissance design to one more in keeping with a Muslim country. The Moorish style has set a tradition for the city's contemporary architects and the nearby Dayabumi skyscraper is a superb example of how Islamic design can be successfully combined with modern forms.

At night, the action centres on Jalan Petaling in the heart of old Chinatown, where the streets are closed off to make way for an outdoor market. Hordes of pedestrians jostle past cassette hawkers and pork-floss vendors; salesmen thrust fake Rolex watches and Gucci T-shirts at tourists, and the night air is pungent with spicy cooking aromas. There is a cacophony

*Kuala Lumpur in 1907, showing the State Secretariat, now the Sultan Abdul Samad Building, soon after its completion.*

of sounds: blind buskers playing Yamaha organs compete with Malay heavy-metal and Chinese opera, and the patter of the fruit vendors extolling the virtues of Californian grapes or Filipino mangoes. In the Chinese language, civilization is known as *reh-nau*, meaning 'hot and noisy', and for devotees of city bustle, Jalan Petaling offers an unabashed look at genuine Chinese street life.

## PENANG

Kuala Lumpur may be Malaysia's capital but it is Penang that retains the kudos as the nation's undisputed top tourist attraction, a reputation it has enjoyed for quite some time judging by a 1930s visitor's remark that compared to other Asian cities Penang was a place where 'Europeans lived by choice'.

Shaped like a turtle, a mere 24 kilometres long by 12 wide (15 by seven and a half miles), Pulau Pinang, as the island is officially known, is located off the northwest coast of Peninsular Malaysia. Blessed with splendid beaches, an ancient port city of bustling bazaars and historical architecture, and a renowned cuisine, Penang still lives up to its old title – 'The Pearl of the Orient'.

Like all romantic port cities Penang's beginnings have inspired some legends. Its founding father, Francis Light, is said to have ordered his ships to fire cannonloads of silver coins into the jungle to inspire his workers to clear the land with more enthusiasm. From its inception in 1786 as the first British-controlled port on the Malay Peninsula, Penang boomed. Light even recommended importing large quantities of opium in order to attract merchants, little knowing that the city's reputation as an easy city in which to procure drugs would endure even to the present day.

An international coterie of traders sailed in to enjoy the duty-free perks, and some of their descendants are part of the island's variegated ethnic mix of today. Chinese form over half of the one-million-strong population, with one-third Malays, and 11 per cent Indians, although this breakdown fails to take into account the diversity of these groups and their cultures. Such variety was first remarked upon by the adventurous Isabella Bird in her book *The Golden Chersonese – Travels in Malaya in 1879*: 'The sight of the Asiatics who have crowded into Georgetown is a wonderful one, Chinese, Burmese, Javanese, Arabs, Malays, Sikhs, Madrassees, Klings, Chuliahs and Parsees, and still they come in junks and steamers and strange Arabian craft, and all get a living, depend slavishly on no one, never lapse into pauperism, retain their own dress, customs, and religion, and are orderly.'

Penangites consider themselves different from mainlanders, no doubt in part because of their geographical separation, although these days a bridge connects the island with the Peninsula. They are often seen as being more independently minded and it is no coincidence that some of the nation's most controversial and outspoken characters come from Penang.

All roads radiate from Georgetown, the capital, which now spreads over most of the north-east of the island, though Francis Light's original grid of streets is still at the city's hub. Many of the thoroughfares still bear English names, although some have recently been changed by the administration, which prefers not to glorify the colonialists. However, the old names may have disappeared from signs but they are still commonly used. Unlike Singapore, its rival port, Penang has kept many of its older buildings, and a walk through the city's streets, lined with 19th-century shophouses and historic temples and mosques, is a journey back through time.

Downtown, beside the sea, is Fort Cornwallis, built by Light to defend the fledgling port, with its fine cannon which apparently were never fired. Facing the fort, flanked by colonial government buildings, is the Padang where expatriates once played cricket, bowls and croquet. To the west along the seafront is the acclaimed Eastern and Oriental Hotel (the 'E & O') where Noel Coward and Somerset Maugham used to stay, and where the Hollywood siren Rita Hayworth sunbathed by the sea.

Penang's multireligious background is evidenced by its wealth of historic houses of worship. The classically elegant St George's Church, built in 1810, is the oldest Anglican church in South-east Asia. The bustling Goddess of Mercy Temple, dating from 1800, is always crammed with Buddhist worshippers, while the Kapitan Kling Mosque, dominated by a towering minaret, dates from about the same time and was built by the then leader of the Indian Muslim community. Penang also boasts Malaysia's most elaborate Chinese clan house, 'The Dragon Mountain Hall', better known as the Khoo Kongsi, with its dragon-adorned roof reputed to weigh over 25 tonnes.

Although far from the best on Malaysia's

coast, Penang's beaches are where the tourists flock to, especially along the north coast where at Batu Feringghi the palm trees have given way to a line of high-rise hotels. Many tourists hardly venture from the beach, and the strip of restaurants and boutiques behind it, which is a pity as Penang has so much more to offer.

### PULAU LANGKAWI

Not so long ago the idyllic islands of Langkawi, 104 in all, which float in the translucent seas of the far north-west, were hardly known to international travellers. Some adventurous backpackers had been coming here for years, but Langkawi was a place in a time-warp, where villagers were more interested in the islands' legends and the annual rice crop than the tourists' dollars, and where it was rare to come across another visitor. And then Langkawi was 'discovered'. Today, tourists fly in on package tours, stay in five-star resorts, eat at fancy restaurants, shop at duty-free emporia, and tool around the newly sealed roads in hire-cars. Villagers who once owned virtually useless coastal properties are now millionaires, and fishermen who formerly lived a hand-to-mouth existence now run lucrative charter services to the outlying islands. However, Langkawi is not all glitz, and much of its picturesque rural scenery survives. In the interior of the main island, village life remains traditional, and most of the smaller islands are uninhabited and deliciously deserted.

Mahsuri, Langkawi's legendary 14th-century heroine who was wrongly accused of adultery and executed, was long thought to have been responsible for the islands' slow development. As she was speared to death she cursed Langkawi for seven generations, a period that coincidentally only recently expired. She is commemorated by a marble tomb which is a favourite domestic tourist site. Many of the islands' other attractions are also woven around with legends, like Tasek Dayang Bunting, 'The Lake of the Pregnant Maiden', where legend has it that a childless woman conceived after 19 years of infertility. But the islands' geographic features are their biggest attraction. Backed by forest-clad mountains with marble cliffs, and draped with palm trees, Langkawi's beaches with their dazzling white sands and waveless seas are picture-postcard perfect, and just the right medicine for a jaded traveller.

### MELAKA – MALAYSIA'S OLDEST TOWN

Located halfway down the Straits of Melaka, the ancient port of Melaka is not only the nation's oldest town, founded 600 years ago, but as the birthplace of the Melakan sultanate it also boasts the most impressive history.

On St Paul's Hill, which rises from the Melaka River in the hub of the original town, a sea-breeze gently ruffles the leaves of the huge tropical trees with their buttress roots and tendril-like epiphytes. Up here there is a ruined Portuguese church where St Francis Xavier was once buried. Below are the solid red buildings constructed by the Dutch, and spreading out on the other side of the river is a sea of red tiled roofs, riddled with the maze of narrow streets that constitutes old Chinatown. It was on St Paul's Hill that the Melaka sultans had their palaces before the European usurpers forced them into exile. Sultan Mansur Shah's magnificent wooden palace, with its seven-tiered roof decorated with gilded spires and covered in copper and zinc shingles, was of such fine workmanship, according to a 15th-century historian, 'that not another royal palace in the world at that time could compare with it'. It was described in such detail that the Melakan State Government has built a replica at the base of St Paul's Hill. This is said to be the largest wooden palace in South-east Asia, although the state's coffers were obviously not as full as they had been in Melaka's heyday: the shingles are of wood not metal, and the beams are not gilded.

When the Portuguese took over they built their immense fortress of A Famosa around the perimeter of St Paul's Hill. Of all the buildings once contained by its mighty walls, only the ruined church of St Paul's and the one surviving gate, Porta de Santiago, remain. A coat-of-arms on this gate is evidence of the subsequent conquerors, the Dutch, who repaired the fort. They also constructed the substantial Stadthuys and the Christ Church which are still the crowning glory of Melaka's Town Square, nicknamed 'The Red Square' after the distinctive shade of the Dutch buildings.

Town houses dating from the Dutch period overhang the river which was once the city's major artery, and despite changing times is still used by visiting Sumatran *praus* whose sailors continue to barter rice for charcoal. When they hoist their great canvas sails and head back to Sumatra, with the trade winds filling their sheets, you could almost imagine Melaka as it was in its days as 'the Queen of the Spice Trade'. Many of the rich merchants' homes, some dating from the Dutch era, are to be found in the two main arteries of old Chinatown, Jalan Tun Tan Cheng Lock (formerly known as Heeren Street), and Jalan Hang Jebat, often called by its old name, Jonkers Street. Styled after South Chinese town houses, these elaborately decorated buildings are still the ancestral homes of many rich Baba families, some of whom have been in Melaka since its earliest days. In Jalan Hang Jebat, dozens of antique shops stock curios and heirlooms from Melaka's chequered past, and the surrounding narrow lanes contain ancient warriors' tombs and some of Malaysia's oldest mosques, as well as the country's oldest Chinese and Indian temples – evidence of the city's historic status.

Around the old heart, and spreading like a cancer about it, is the new city of Melaka, full of concrete rows of houses, and ugly contemporary buildings, including a few high-rise hotels. Housing estates built on reclaimed land stretch out to engulf the coastline where the sea once lapped at the kitchen doors of palatial Heeren Street houses. There are huge new industrial estates and even a petroleum complex, but for all these changes Melaka still has an aura about it. The villages surrounding the city retain some of Malaysia's most traditional houses. Surrounded by rice paddies and palm trees, they seem to have defied the march of time. And with record numbers of tourists coming to see Melaka's tangible reminders of her glorious history, today's administration is very much aware of the need to conserve what remains for the future.

### HILL RESORTS – THE COOL ESCAPE

Coming from temperate realms, the British colonialists were always looking for somewhere to escape from the stifling heat of the lowlands. From Ceylon to India and Burma, colonial adventurers slogged up hills and mountains in order to create their 'hill stations' where not only could they take a break in cooler climes, and walk and play sports without being drenched in perspiration, but they could create little pockets of the old country to assuage their homesickness. Malaysia was no different, and from the beginning of British dominion government surveyors were sent off to explore the highlands, not only to gauge the land, but to look for possible sites for hill retreats.

The oldest is Bukit Larut, formerly Maxwell's Hill, named after the British Resident who first mooted the idea of a resort here in the late 19th century. In the early days visitors either walked along a jungle path or took the advice of an early guide book and contacted Taik Ho & Co. of Taiping, in the nearby town, who could 'provide chairs and coolies for people wishing to go up the hills'. These days, a jeep trail winds to the top of the hill, 1,035 metres (3,400 feet) high, but not much else has changed. The cottages set amongst dahlia gardens on terraced lawns look much as they must have in colonial days. There is no commercial development, and little to do but look at the views of Perak's coast and explore the surrounding forest.

Lower in altitude but higher in popularity, Penang Hill is only a paltry 731 metres (2,400 feet) above sea-level. The weekend queues to board the trains on the funicular railway to the summit attest to its status as a top tourist destination. Penangites are fiercely protective of their hill – a recent plan to modernize the colonial-style retreat, turning it into a theme-park and luxury resort, was adamantly opposed. Francis Light, the founding father, built the first bungalow on Strawberry Hill (where he grew the colony's first strawberries) and other moneyed Penangites followed his example. Trails wind past these retreats and pockets of intervening forest, tea-houses serve Devonshire teas, and the Bellevue Hotel still welcomes guests as it did early this century when the novelist Hermann Hesse walked up the trail from the Botanic Gardens and called in for a drink.

Cameron Highlands, named after the surveyor who discovered this lofty region, is Malaysia's largest and best-known hill retreat. At an altitude of between 1,500 and 1,800 metres (4,900 and 5,900 feet), the highlands encompass the towns of Ringlet, Tanah Rata, and Brinchang which are surrounded by terraced vegetable farms, tea plantations, and forest-clad mountains. While Bukit Larut and Penang Hill are usually visited on day trips, Cameron Highlands is a popular holiday destination for both domestic and international travellers. In the hills around Tanah Rata are colonial-style bungalows and luxury retreats – the haunts of the rich, royal and famous of Malaysian society. Ye Olde Smokehouse is the ultimate in colonial nostalgia. This 50-year-old, Tudor-style hotel is draped with ivy and flanked by rose-gardens. It serves strawberries and cream on the terrace and traditional roasts at night by a roaring log fire. Walking trails wind through the surrounding hills which are covered in dense montane rainforests, where pitcher plants and rhododendrons grow on the cloud-shrouded summits.

Bukit Fraser (Fraser's Hill), named after a mysterious mule-train operator who ran a tin mine in the vicinity and then disappeared, is a favourite destination for Kuala Lumpur residents. Renowned for its prolific bird-life, and the lushness of the surrounding forest, this cool resort is located 1,500 metres (4,900 feet) up in the Banjaran Titiwangsa.

Ironically, W.E. Maxwell, the British Resident who founded the first hill station, lamented that the native races were not as enamoured of hill stations as the British were. These days, anyone who has tried to obtain a hotel room in any of these resorts over holiday seasons when they are crowded with Malaysian and Singaporean tourists, could not fail to observe that if the British Resident could see these retreats now he would certainly rue his words. In his day it was not a question of whether the indigenous people liked them or not, it was merely that their economic situation did not allow for leisure time. Times have changed, however, and now ordinary Malaysians can afford these pleasures. The British left them the architecture and the format and started the ball rolling. Now the rustic hotels, the rose-gardens and the tea plantations are unmistakably Malaysian, part of the fabric of their history, and very much a part of the present.

## THE EAST COAST – MALAY HEARTLAND

On a sun-drenched strand of Kelantan's north coast, a group of fishermen, wearing sarongs and batik headgear, are chanting while with straining muscles they pull a rainbow-coloured boat out of the surf and up onto rollers made of coconut trunks on the beach. Offshore, bobbing in the surf, are a score more of these elaborately decorated boats, and within the hour they will all be beached, the catch will be sorted, and the fishermen's wives – wearing armloads of golden bangles in characteristic Kelantanese style – will be haggling prices with the fishmongers who have been coming to Kampung Dasar Sabak for generations. This beach, famed for its colourful *bangau* boats, provides a spectacle which is unique to Kelantan, but there are dozens of other east coast beaches and estuaries where fishermen still take to the sea in boats that are not quite as spectacular but are just as traditional. However, scenes like this are rare on the west coast, as are the other highlights of the predominantly Malay east coast, with its villages where time-honoured crafts are still pursued, and where traditional sports like top-spinning and kite-flying are still enjoyed.

The geography of Malaysia explains why the east coast is so different from the west. The mountainous interior served as an effective barrier between the two coasts, as did the absence of protected harbours and the annual monsoon, which often kept ships docked for months at a time. While the British were busily clearing the west coast for plantations, and bringing in thousands of workers for these and the tin mines, the east coast states of Kelantan and Terengganu were still loosely under the sovereignty of the Thai court, and as a result were not so exploited. Pahang had secured a similar arrangement to Johor (see page 30) and was for a while independent, with Sultan Ahmad stressing that he would rather see his state revert to a jungle than let it be governed by the British. However, by threats and coercion a British Resident was finally planted in Pahang in 1888. But the bulk of the population was not convinced. The resulting rebellion known as the Pahang War, led by the charismatic Mat Kilau, although only a brief setback, was a thorn in the side of the British. The colonialists had thought Pahang was a land of incredible mineral riches, but they had failed to take its geographical difficulties into account. Its lode tin was more difficult to access than the alluvial deposits of the west, and the boat trip from Singapore up the Pahang River to the colonial capital of Kuala Lipis took a fortnight. The state's economy was always in the red, and because the Chinese immigrants preferred the west coast, the Malay character of the state remained.

Kelantan and Terengganu were even more difficult of access. Although a railway was constructed through the interior of the east coast to Kelantan in the 1930s, and a road was built across the ranges to Kuantan from Kuala Lumpur, a direct route to Kelantan from the west coast came into existence only in 1982 when the East-West Highway was completed. This knocked 600 kilometres (370 miles) off the road distance between Penang and Kota Bharu. Ironically, although the east still lags behind the west in living standards, the huge petroleum and gas deposits discovered off the Terengganu coast have been one of the main reasons behind Malaysia's economic boom of the past decade.

Kelantan, 'the land of lightning', is renowned for its fertile rice fields, golden beaches, picturesque fishing villages, and its arts and crafts and traditional performances. Kota Bharu, the state capital and the royal seat, sprawls along the east bank of the Kelantan River which often floods during the monsoon. In the historical centre of town are old wooden palaces converted into museums of royalty and culture, which show the superb craftsmanship of Kelantan's wood-carvers, and a central market which has no equal in all Malaysia for colour, excitement, and for its incredible variety of fruits and vegetables. Silk-weavers, batik-makers, silversmiths, kite-makers, and wood-carvers ply their trades in the villages surrounding the town. In Kota Bharu's cultural centre visitors can view top-spinning, *rebana ubi* (giant-drum) competitions, *silat* (Malay self-defence), and shadow puppet performances.

Terengganu's beaches are legendary, as are the giant turtles that lumber up the sands at Rantau Abang to lay their eggs every year. Kuala Terengganu, the capital and seat of royalty, is an ancient port overlooking the river estuary after which it is named. Islam first came to Malaysia at the upriver town of Kuala Berang, as is evidenced by the Terengganu Stone, inscribed with Muslim laws predating Melaka's conversion, which was discovered by a 19th-century Arab trader. Terengganu is still a bastion of the faith and its religious schools are famed throughout the region.

Offshore from both Terengganu and Pahang are scores of tropical islands which are popular retreats for both domestic and international tourists. The incomparable, mountainous Pulau Tioman achieved fame as the setting for the film *South Pacific*. Pulau Perhentian is renowned for its dazzling white sands and aquamarine waters, and pocket-sized Pulau Rawa for its well-known resort run by Johorean royalty. Dozens of other islands run the gamut from rocky outcrops to the archetypal tropical paradise, where a traveller can lie on a palm-draped beach, indulge in a fresh coconut drink, and feel that this is surely the way life was meant to be.

## TAMAN NEGARA – THE NATIONAL PARK

Its name translating simply as 'The National Park', Taman Negara is Malaysia's oldest and largest protected tract of rainforest, covering 4,343 square kilometres (1,677 square miles) of the backlands of the states of Kelantan, Pahang and Terengganu. Dominating the mountainous ridge which bisects the park from east to west is Gunung Tahan, the highest peak on the Peninsula at 2,187 metres (7,175 feet), where climbers can journey through every type of Malaysian forest, from lowland and montane rainforests to the mossy 'cloud forests' at the summit. Lowland forest trees tower up to 45 metres (150 feet) high, as the park has been off limits to loggers ever since it was established as a sanctuary in 1937, and rivers run pure and unmuddied. Most of the country's most famous mammals including Tigers, Elephants, *seladang* (wild ox), Tapirs, and Honey Bears are still prevalent in Taman Negara. However, owing to the dense tree cover, their shyness with humans, their excellent sensory organs, their nocturnal habits and their uncanny ability to camouflage themselves, most large mammals are difficult to spot unless travellers are prepared to hike into the untrodden depths of the park. The best way to see smaller mammals like deer, civets, and occasionally larger animals like *seladang* and Tapir, is to stay overnight at one of the hides which are located close to salt-licks where the animals are often seen. Wild pigs, deer, and sometimes even the miniature Mouse-deer come right up to the lawns by the chalets, and this is also an excellent place to view much of the park's huge variety of bird-life. Up to 200 species of fish live in the rivers and streams of Taman Negara and there are upriver fishing lodges where keen anglers can stay while they try to hook the fighting Kelah or the Kelesa, which is known for its ability to leap high out of the water.

Taman Negara is not an easy place to get to, which is probably one of the reasons that it has managed to retain such a primeval aura. Travellers must first journey to Kuala Tembeling in the interior of Pahang. From there the 59-kilometre (37-mile) boat journey up the Tembeling River takes about four hours – longer in the dry season – to Park Headquarters at Kuala Tahan. Here there is accommodation to suit all tastes, and restaurants where tired trekkers can even reward themselves with ice-cream. Outside, though, there is only the forest. Some visitors are overawed by its sheer immensity: the cloying humidity, and the occasional leech bite, are enough to discourage the faint-hearted. But they have to walk only a short distance to swim in crystal-clear streams, or take a boat-ride through the rapids, and the easy walking trails around Headquarters provide a unique insight into some of the world's oldest rainforests. For the more adventurous, trails wind through much of the park's interior, and for those who are fit enough, the gruelling nine-day trek to the summit of Gunung Tahan is a once-in-a-lifetime experience.

## KUCHING AND SARAWAK'S UPRIVER SAFARIS

The *tambang* boats with names like 'Everlasting Cannon' are jostling for position at the wooden jetty beside the khaki-coloured Sarawak River. The folk from the

*Demonstrating a fire-making technique in a Kayan longhouse in 1905. The method involved rubbing a cane thong against a piece of soft wood.*

other side of the river disembark and mount the stairs to the market where an Iban stripped to the waist cuts up sides of beef with an axe, a young woman squats on the floor and carves up a huge jackfruit, and a Melanau youth shoulders a metre-long bundle of yellow fronds from the Nipa palm to be used for rolling traditional cigarettes. The *tambang* fills up for the return trip and the boatman casts off, motors slightly upstream, then turns the engine off and drifts down to the other shore in the current. He docks in front of an unusual building with a steep thatched roof and two battlemented square towers. On the lawn that slopes to the river, clipped hedges spell out 'Astana', the Malay word for 'palace', as this quaint building was once the residence of Sarawak's 'White Rajahs', who ruled the state for over a century from their power base here in Kuching.

Located 32 kilometres (20 miles) upstream from where the Sarawak River empties into the South China Sea, the state capital of Kuching was founded by the Englishman James Brooke, who had the great good fortune to acquire much of Sarawak as his own personal fief in 1841. How the capital acquired its name, which means 'cat' in Malay, is the subject of various theories. According to local lore, when Brooke was meeting with the native chiefs a cat dashed across the room and, hearing its name in their dialect, he chose it for the town. A look-out tower has been built in parkland beside the Astana, and from the top there is a bird's eye vista of modern Kuching. Malay *kampung* houses, high on stilts, dominate this northern side of the river while on the other bank is the commercial heart of Kuching. The markets hug the shoreline, and behind them are the glowing domes of the State Mosque. Upstream are more historical buildings from the Rajah's day, and behind them, the rectangular towers of luxury hotels. Dominating the horizon in the distance is a table-shaped peak standing alone and to the right are the ranges that separate Indonesian Kalimantan from Sarawak.

Dragons like sea-serpents writhe in a cobalt-blue sea around the wall frieze which encircles Kuching's oldest Chinese temple, Tua Pek Kong, perched in a commanding position overlooking the river in the centre of Chinatown. At festival time, hawkers sell joss-sticks and bunches of chrysanthemums. Devotees pray to the gods in the red-painted temple, asking that they favour their businesses with good returns, and give them healthy sons who are clever enough to go to university. Chinese traders had been coming to Sarawak for centuries before the era of the 'White Rajahs', and Hakkas controlled the rich gold-mining area of Bau before James Brooke even set foot in Kuching. Not keen to submit to British rule, they attacked the town and reduced the Malay quarter to ashes in 1857, but the Malays, Iban, and the Chinese clans opposed to the Hakka suppressed the uprising. Chinese immigration was encouraged by the Brooke regime for economic reasons and as a result Sarawak's Chinese population today is around one-third of the total.

Kuching is famous all over South-east Asia, and amongst Borneophiles the world over, for its museum. The collection was started by the second Rajah Charles Brooke in collaboration with the naturalist Alfred Russel Wallace. A contemporary of Darwin, Wallace independently developed a virtually identical theory of evolution mainly as a result of his Bornean discoveries. Traditional artefacts and displays on the lifestyles of Sarawak's indigenous people, and animals stuffed in the Victorian fashion, make for an absorbing visit. There are all kinds of oddities to amuse and entrance, such as a cannonball-sized hairball from a crocodile's stomach which when found included a human dental plate; a wooden press used for flattening the foreheads of Melanau children; and the wooden propeller of the first plane to land in Sarawak in 1924.

Kuching is the jumping-off spot for upriver safaris into the lands of the Iban, and the Kayan and Kenyah. Skrang River is the closest of these areas (four hours by car and one by boat from Kuching) and the longhouses here give a fascinating insight into traditional Iban life. Further afield, up Malaysia's longest river, the Rajang, express boats dock at Kapit, 160 kilometres (100 miles) upstream, before leaving Iban country for Belaga, the heartland of the Kayan and Kenyah peoples. On the way to Belaga are the notorious Pelagus rapids, seven in all, which are a constant hazard but provide the local boatmen with an opportunity to show off their prowess, for which they are justifiably famous.

The further upstream one travels, the more traditional are the lifestyles and the longhouses, as though time was measured by the distance from civilization. An evening spent watching a tribal elder perform the hornbill dance by the light of a flickering lantern, far from the nearest town, is just one of Sarawak's memorable experiences.

## MULU AND NIAH – SARAWAK'S GREAT CAVERNS

In the far north of the state, accessible from the oil town of Miri, are two national parks famed for their enormous cave systems, some of the world's longest and largest. The nearer is Niah National Park, 96 kilometres (60 miles) south of Miri. According to legend, the inhabitants of Niah turned to stone and the houses into caves when a grandmother turned her curses on the villagers for sacrificing her grandchild under the centre-pole of a new longhouse in order to appease the gods.

From Park Headquarters a short boat ride brings visitors to a boardwalk raised above the forest floor to protect the delicate ecology of the region. Winding past huge rainforest trees with buttress roots and draped with lianas, the trail arrives at a limestone massif that contains the aptly named Great Cave, where in 1958 Tom Harrisson, curator of the Sarawak Museum, dug up a human skull dating back 35,000 years. High up on the ceiling are nests made of swiftlets' saliva and the flimsy bamboo scaffolding used by the death-defying collectors of this highly priced delicacy favoured by Chinese gourmets. According to historians, Niah natives, who deserted the caves in about 1400, had been selling birds' nests and hornbill ivory (from the casque of the Helmeted Hornbill) to Chinese traders since the seventh century. Huge mounds of guano formed from centuries of swiftlets' and bats' droppings form the undulating floor of the Great Cave. A trail winds up and over these hills of excreta to the Painted Cave, where red haematite wall-paintings were discovered in 1958, the only cave-paintings found in Borneo. Beside them are tiny wooden canoes at least 1,200 years old, which were used as coffins or 'ships of the dead'.

Gunung Mulu National Park takes a full day's river journey to reach, but the trip up the mighty Baram River, past longhouses and 'cowboy' timber towns, with Penan and Kenyah fellow passengers, is almost as good as what is in store at the end. At Long Panai the express boat is exchanged for a wooden longboat for the journey up the Tutoh River, then up the Melinau, the first of the wild rivers, with none of the muddiness of Sarawak's other streams.

Gunung Mulu, Sarawak's highest peak, dominates the horizon, flanked by sugar-loaf hills streaked with white limestone and riddled by the great caves. Upstream, the Melinau's progress is abruptly stopped by a huge limestone cliff. When Spencer St John ventured here in 1856, the first European to do so, he thought that this was where the river began. Little did he realize that this was the start of South-east Asia's longest cave system. The trail through the Clearwater Cave sometimes crosses the river, which was responsible for gouging out the entire system, 50 kilometres (31 miles) long. After one and a half kilometres (one mile), or a three-hour walk inside, ferns and creepers cascade through a hole in the roof where sunlight breaks into the gloom – from here on the only light is provided by torches.

Deer Cave is as large as Clearwater is long. Two kilometres (one and a quarter miles) long with a ceiling that is never lower than 100 metres (330 feet), its entrance boasts spectacular waterfalls which cascade 190 metres (625 feet) to the floor below. A trek over guano hills and via a rope-ladder descent emerges into the enchanted Garden of Eden, a hidden valley framed by the cavernous eastern end of the Deer Cave.

About 900 metres (2,950 feet) up Gunung Api, another peak in Gunung Mulu National Park, is a mountainside of needle-pointed limestone pinnacles which rise 45 metres (150 feet), towering above the treetops and described by Spencer St John as 'the world's most nightmarish surface to travel over'. A climb to Gunung Mulu's summit entails a five-day expedition and more than average fitness, while the Sarawak Chamber, the park's *pièce de résistance*, is reputedly the world's largest cave chamber – about the size of 16 football fields – but is not yet open to the public.

## KOTA KINABALU AND SABAH'S GREAT MOUNTAIN

Known as 'The Land Below the Wind' because it lies south of the typhoon belt, Sabah is not only the setting for Malaysia's highest mountain, but has spectacular national and marine parks, a fascinating Orang-utan sanctuary, and a diverse and colourful population.

Kota Kinabalu, the capital, has little to offer of historical interest, having been razed to the ground during the Second World War, but it serves as a pleasant base for the state's geographical attractions.

Offshore from the city are the five islands which comprise the Tunku Abdul Rahman Park, where divers can explore the coral reefs, and nature-lovers can spot crab-eating monkeys and Pied Hornbills. Kinabalu Park is named after the mountain, 4,101 metres (13,455 feet) high, which dominates the surrounding country. Its spiritual significance for the local Kadazan people is easily understood by anyone who has the privilege to view this awesome peak. The summit trail takes the climber through a range of different ecosystems from dense montane rainforest, through a natural arena covered in moss and shrouded with cloud, to the bonsai plants of the higher realms and the great granite summit plateau. Climbs are organized so that the summit is gained just before dawn, in order to see the spectacular sunrise creeping across Sabah at your feet. Less adventurous travellers can explore the many trails around Park Headquarters, admire the flowering rhododendrons – many species are unique to the park – and relax in the cool, bracing climate which is a relief from the stifling lowlands. Weary climbers are advised to take a hot mineral bath at the Poring Springs, where the world's largest flower, the *Rafflesia*, grows in the surrounding forest.

Across the ranges, near Sandakan, is the Sepilok Forest Reserve where Orang-utans rescued from captivity are rehabilitated and then released into the wild. This is a lengthy process, as Orang-utan young can only learn by watching other apes. Also on the outskirts of Sandakan are the Gomantong Caves, where the agile Orang Sungai clamber about the ceilings to collect prized edible birds' nests, and offshore are islands where Green and Hawksbill Turtles come ashore to lay their eggs.

In the remote south-east of Sabah is the colourful and lively port of Semporna, home base of the Bajau, or 'sea gypsies', and the jumping-off spot for Malaysia's best scuba-diving. At Pulau Sipadan, the remnant of an ancient volcanic crater, the turquoise waters plunge off an underwater cliff-face 600 metres (1970 feet) high, where the coral is outstanding and the sea-life prolific.

# The Land

An artist moving from Europe to Malaysia once said that at home there were only half a dozen greens that he could distinguish but that in these lush tropical realms there were at least 50 – enough to inspire him for a lifetime.

The hothouse atmosphere which prevails all year round in the lowlands – a combination of high temperatures, soaring humidity and abundant rainfall – fosters the overwhelming greenness of the Malaysian countryside. From the mangroves on the coastal fringe, through the rice paddies of the plains, to the towering rainforests of the interior – all is fecund green.

Fringed with coconut palms, ribbons of white sandy beaches predominate on the Peninsula's east coast. Offshore, tropical islands like Pulau Tioman, renowned for its clear waters and towering forests, bejewel the South China Sea. The mountainous spine of the Peninsula still harbours vast tracts of rainforests, including those of Taman Negara, the National Park, safeguarding a wealth of plant and animal species, and culminating in Gunung Tahan, the Peninsula's highest mountain. On the western watershed are the famed hill resorts including Cameron Highlands with its terraced tea plantations. In the northwest, limestone massifs pitted with caves rear sheer-sided from the lime-green rice fields; around Ipoh, many of these caves house Buddhist temples.

Sabah and Sarawak, the Bornean states, are even more geographically splendid, containing not only immense tracts of rainforest, but Malaysia's longest rivers and highest mountains, including lofty Mount Kinabalu. Ecosystems range from mangrove wetlands, coastal heath forests, and the tropical rainforests of the lowlands to montane oak forests where ferns garland the moss-covered trees, and stark alpine realms with the tiniest of dwarf rhododendrons and orchids flowering like snow drifts in the rock crevices.

*Creating a leafy canopy, the virginal rainforest of Taman Negara, Malaysia's oldest and largest national park, escaped the threat of logging when it was declared a reserve in 1937. The rivers inside the park still run clear, their waters unaffected by the silting that logging causes, and totally different from the milk-chocolate-coloured water of most of the country's rivers. This region contains some of the world's oldest rainforests. Those of the Congo and the Amazon are young by comparison.*

PREVIOUS PAGES: Page 58. Above left: *Sunset gilds the clouds rising up the slopes of Mount Kinabalu in Sabah.* Above right: *One of the numerous waterfalls in Lambir Hills National Park near Miri in Sarawak.* Below left: *Immensely tall and with relatively shallow roots, mature dipterocarp trees may develop huge supporting buttresses like this example in Niah National Park, Sarawak.* Below right: *Early morning on a beach in Penang.*
Page 59: *Flowers of* Bauhinia kockiana, *a climbing plant in the forest in Lambir Hills National Park.*

*The prolific rainfall of this equatorial region promotes lush vegetation in the rainforests of Taman Negara, a vast protected area straddling the interior of Pahang, Kelantan and Terengganu states. This vast quantity of water collects in numerous rivers like the Tahan* (above left), *which originates from Gunung Tahan, Peninsular Malaysia's highest mountain at 2,187 metres (7,175 feet), and joins the Tembeling River at Kuala Tahan. In the depths of the rainforest, the dense tree canopy shuts out the tropical sunlight and leaves the forest floor in permanent twilight, enlivened by the glowing red flowers of wild ginger plants* (far left), *and the fruits of palms* (above) *and rattan* (middle left). *This plant is a hazard for hikers as its sharp thorns catch on clothing and skin, but it is one of the world's most versatile plants, providing the raw materials for baskets, mats, blinds and furniture. Where a gap in the canopy allows sunlight to filter through, seedlings soon spring up to cover the ground* (left).

*Pulau Pinang, or Penang as it is universally known, off the north-west coast of Peninsular Malaysia, rose to fame as the 'Pearl of the Orient' during its heyday as an entrepôt early in the 19th century. Its reputation as a tourist attraction has never been eclipsed. To arrive in the grand style, travellers may journey aboard the luxury 'Eastern & Oriental Express'* (above left and right), *which runs weekly between Singapore, Kuala Lumpur and Bangkok, alighting at Butterworth to catch the Penang ferry. Georgetown, the state capital* (left), *sprawls across the north-west corner of the island. The grid layout of the streets is a legacy of colonial days, and the red-tiled roofs cover 19th-century versions of South Chinese shophouses that are an evocative reminder of Penang's colourful history. They stand in stark contrast to the island's highest building, the soaring KOMTAR office tower from which this photograph was taken.*

*Fine buildings from the Victorian colonial era still survive along the northern coastline, surrounded by lawns and manicured gardens* (above), *though others have succumbed to the sledgehammer and have been replaced with luxury hotels and condominiums. Penang Clocktower* (above right), *beside Georgetown's ferry terminal, is built in a Moorish style that is characteristic of Peninsular architecture during the late 19th century. A Chinese tycoon, one of many who became exceedingly wealthy during the rubber boom, financed the building of this tiered edifice in honour of Queen Victoria's Jubilee celebrations in 1897.*

Right: *Penang has been a favourite travel destination for decades and its picturesque northern beaches are a major reason for its popularity.*

Above: *The rosy flush of an equatorial dawn signals a new day over scenic Pulau Langkawi, the largest of a group of 104 islands located off the far north-west coast of Peninsular Malaysia near the Thai border.*

Left: *Deserted beaches lapped by warm peaceful waters make these islands a Mecca for tourists, although only a decade or so ago they were hardly known on the international travellers' circuit.*

Above right: *Towering limestone hills, their sheer cliffs riddled with caves, are a distinctive feature of the islands. In the north-east of Pulau Langkawi marble quarried in these hills is turned into table-tops, vases and floors for luxury bathrooms.*

Right: *Mineral deposits darken the coral sand at the aptly-named Pantai Pasir Hitam (Beach of Black Sand) on the north coast of Pulau Langkawi.*

Opposite: *Rubber trees, characteristically planted in geometric avenues, are found in plantations in Pulau Langkawi's interior, but their economic importance has declined in the wake of the islands' tourism boom.*

Above: *On Pulau Dayang Bunting, the second largest of the Langkawi islands, is Tasek Dayang Bunting, which takes its name, 'the Lake of the Pregnant Maiden', from a local legend of the 18th century. A woman who had been childless for 19 years apparently bathed in the lake's waters and not long afterwards conceived. Its crystal-clear waters are delightfully cool and are a favourite bathing-place for islanders and tourists alike.*

Right: *Despite the recent additions of luxury hotels and increasing tourist numbers, Pulau Langkawi still has picturesque rural countryside where water buffalo contentedly graze under towering coconut palms.*

*Montane forests shroud the Malaysian highlands growing above 800 metres (2,600 feet) and up to about 1,700 metres (5,600 feet) above sea level. The forest shown here* (left) *is in the vicinity of Genting Highlands. These damp forests, often covered in cloud, are the perfect environment for a huge variety of plant life, including orchids* (above). *On the Peninsula alone there are no less than 800 different species which grow from the seaboard to the highest mountain peaks.*

Above: *Spectacular montane forest at Fraser's Hill, a small resort town in the Main Range about two hours' drive from Kuala Lumpur.*

Right: *On terraces cut from the hillsides of Cameron Highlands, market gardens provide most of the vegetables not only for Peninsular Malaysia but also for Singapore.*

FOLLOWING PAGES
*Tea estates cloak the hills around Brinchang in the Cameron Highlands. Those of Boh Tea, Malaysia's best-known brand, are still owned and run by the descendants of the Englishman J. A. Russell who first opened up the district in the 1930s.*

Above: *Keyhole archways create a marvellous, Islamic-inspired corridor at the Railway Administration Building, one of Kuala Lumpur's renowned Moorish buildings from the British colonial period. Another is the splendid* Sultan Abdul Samad Building (below right) *with its gleaming copper domes and central clocktower. The legacy of the British era also includes cricket, still played on the Padang in front of the half-timbered Royal Selangor Club* (above right).

Opposite: *It is hard to imagine that Kuala Lumpur, Malaysia's fast-growing capital city, was only a struggling mining settlement not much more than a century ago. Home to at least 1.5 million people – a figure that is constantly being revised – the city is now expanding upwards. Towering over the older colonial areas of Kuala Lumpur are many architecturally acclaimed contemporary skyscrapers.*

Above: *Officially known as the Masjid Sultan Salahuddin, the Selangor State Mosque located in Shah Alam, the state capital only half an hour's drive from Kuala Lumpur, is not only the largest building of its kind in South-east Asia, but its dome, which measures 91 metres (299 feet) high and 52 metres (171 feet) wide, is one of the world's largest. It was completed in 1988 at a cost of RM160 million and can accommodate 16,000 worshippers.*

Left: *Situated where the Kelang River meets the Melaka Straits, Port Kelang has always been the principal seaport for Kuala Lumpur. Before it was linked to the capital by rail in 1885 the river provided the only means of transport.*

*Known variously as the Dutch Square, the Town Square or the Red Square (from the colour of its buildings), this area of downtown Melaka contains some of Malaysia's most historic buildings. To the right is the Stadthuys, once the home of the Dutch governor and now a museum, which was built in 1650; in the middle background is Christ Church, also built by the Dutch in 1753; and to the left is the Clocktower constructed by Tan Beng Swee, a wealthy Straits Chinese businessman, in 1886.*

Above: *Melaka's outskirts are renowned for their traditional Malay houses, like the century-old Penghulu's House at Merlimau, 23 kilometres (14 miles) south of Melaka town. Built by Malay carpenters in 1894 for a village chieftain, the house features a magnificent front staircase covered in art nouveau tiles, ornate woodcarvings and a central courtyard. The descendants of the original owner still live in the house and welcome visitors who appreciate traditional architecture.*

Left: *On St Paul's Hill in the centre of Melaka stand the ruins of the church of Sao Paulo which gave the hill its name. Constructed in 1521 by the Portuguese, who wrested the famous port from the Melakan sultanate, the church stands on the site of the sultans' palace. Inside, an empty crypt once contained the body of St Francis Xavier who is commemorated by a statue. The white tower is a lighthouse, erected by the British in the 19th century.*

Above and right: *Covering 93,000 hectares (360 square miles) and straddling the interior of both Johor and Pahang states, Endau-Rompin is the newest of Malaysia's forest reserves. Rich in plant and animal life, this region is also home to Malaysia's largest population of the endangered Sumatran Rhinoceros. Plateaux and mesas have been formed by sedimentary rocks which overlay older bedrock, causing sharp drops in elevation and resulting in spectacular waterfalls. Much of the Endau-Rompin region is virgin rainforest and new species have recently been discovered, like the Livingstone Fan Palm,* Livistona endauensis (above far right). *The rich flora includes orchids like the Bamboo Orchid,* Arundina graminifolia (below right), *and carnivorous pitcher plants which live off the nutrients obtained from decomposing insects which fall into their 'pitchers'* (Nepenthes ampullaria, below far right).

*Sailing ships have been putting in to Pulau Tioman, a mountainous island 32 kilometres (20 miles) off the coast of Pahang, for at least a thousand years. Marked on ancient Chinese sailing charts, the island provided safe anchorage, plentiful fresh water, plants to make ropes, and game to stock the ships' galleys. In the south of the island, the twin peaks of Batu Sirau and Nenek Si-Mukut* (left), *rearing over 900 metres (2,950 feet) above sea level, were unmistakable navigational beacons on the old trade route which connected China with the Spice Islands and beyond to Europe. White sand beaches* (right), *clear waters, an undisturbed rainforest interior and a laid-back lifestyle are some of the reasons why Pulau Tioman was recently voted in the top ten of the world's most beautiful islands.*

*A paradise for divers and travellers seeking a peaceful beach holiday, Pulau Redang is the largest island in this archipelago 50 kilometres (31 miles) east of Kuala Terengganu in the South China Sea. Talcum-powder sands backed by a forest of coconut palms provide the perfect Robinson Crusoe setting, and the offshore rocky islets offer the best scuba-diving in the region. Villagers live mainly by fishing* (right), *but all this is due to change shortly when the island's billion-dollar resort is completed. As the waters around these islands are some of Malaysia's most pristine, environmental groups are closely monitoring the construction as some experts fear that the island's ecosystems will be adversely affected if strict controls are not maintained.*

*Sunset paints a golden glow over the Sarawak River which divides the city of Kuching, the capital of the East Malaysian state of Sarawak* (left). *Roads now penetrate the interior but the rivers are still major trading arteries. Kuching owes its existence to the adventurous Englishman, James Brooke, first of the 'White Rajahs' who ruled Sarawak from 1841 until the end of World War II. Fort Marguerita* (above), *named after the wife of the second rajah, Charles Brooke, is situated on the northern bank of the river. Traditional boats known as* tambang *still act as ferries plying across the Sarawak River from the commercial side of Kuching to the distinctive Astana* (right), *the original home of the Brooke dynasty which now serves as the residence of the State Governor.*

*Although greatly depleted by logging in the last few decades, Borneo's vast forests are legion and range from coastal mangroves through lowland and montane rainforests up to the bonsai plants of the alpine realms. Sarawak has set aside large forested areas as national parks and reserves. On the Samunsam River in western Sarawak* (opposite above) *Nipa, a trunkless palm used for thatching roofs, lines the banks, its sculptural fruits hanging over the water* (opposite left). *The sandy coast is also the habitat of the cycad,* Cycas rumphii (opposite centre), *a living plant fossil from the age of the dinosaurs. Bako National Park near Kuching* (above) *is characterized by low-growing, compact heath forests. It also contains a picturesque coastline with sandy bays, and forests of mangrove* (opposite right and right), *dipterocarp and peat-swamp.*

FOLLOWING PAGES

*The Sarawak coast at Santubong, a peninsula north of Kuching which has been a stopping-place for traders and explorers in this region since the first millennium.*

Above: *Sibu, Sarawak's upstart boom town, owes its existence to the logging industry. Situated on the Rajang River, Malaysia's longest waterway, the town is connected by road from the capital, Kuching, but commuters usually arrive by express boats or by air rather than take the long road journey. With a population of over 130,000, Sibu is Sarawak's second largest town. Barges groaning with timber are a common sight on the Rajang* (left) *which is navigable by large boats up to Kapit, 160 kilometres (100 miles) upstream.*

Opposite: *A massive strangling fig plant in Gunung Mulu National Park: the host tree around which it grew up has long since died. Sarawak's forests once stretched unimpeded and virginal across most of its 123,985 square kilometres (77,045 square miles), but logging has left its mark and vast areas have been decimated. However, pressure is now being felt and the government is gradually easing up and improving its environmental record.*

Top: *The craggy silhouette of Gunung Mulu, 2,371 metres (7,779 feet) high, which gives the Gunung Mulu National Park its name, dominates the skyline above the forests of the Tutoh River in the north-east of Sarawak. The park is renowned for its mountains and their vast cave systems.*

Above: *This* Clerodendrum paniculatum, *commonly known as a Pagoda Flower, grows around Gunung Mulu National Park and is used by the Penan people as an aphrodisiac.*

Left: *The Great Deer Cave is the world's largest cave passage. At its eastern entrance* (pictured) *the beautiful forest known as the Garden of Eden is framed in the cave's mouth.*

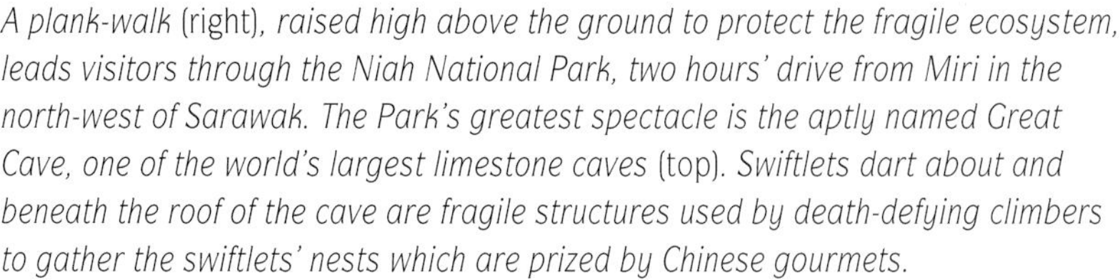

*A plank-walk* (right), *raised high above the ground to protect the fragile ecosystem, leads visitors through the Niah National Park, two hours' drive from Miri in the north-west of Sarawak. The Park's greatest spectacle is the aptly named Great Cave, one of the world's largest limestone caves* (top). *Swiftlets dart about and beneath the roof of the cave are fragile structures used by death-defying climbers to gather the swiftlets' nests which are prized by Chinese gourmets.*

Above: *In 1958, archaeologists discovered these rock paintings at Niah. They are thought to have been drawn around 1,200 years ago by the mysterious Niah people who deserted the caves in the 15th century.*

Above and left: *Kota Kinabalu, the capital of Sabah in East Malaysia, is one of the country's newest cities as it was largely destroyed by bombing in World War II. Then known as Jesselton, it was renamed in 1967 after the majestic mountain that towers in the background. With over 100,000 inhabitants, Kota Kinabalu makes up for its lack of tangible history by its splendid geographical setting.*

Opposite: *Dominating the horizon of much of the northern territory of Sabah, Mount Kinabalu, at a height of 4,101 metres (13,455 feet), is the highest mountain in South-east Asia. Seen here from Kota Belud, the mountain takes its name from the indigenous Kadazan title which means 'The Revered Place of the Dead'.*

*Kinabalu National Park which surrounds the mountain supports a huge variety of plants. Over half the plants growing above 912 metres (3,000 feet) are found nowhere else in the world. Amongst the lush vegetation on the lower slopes of the mountain* (left) *temperate species such as wild raspberries (*Rubus rosaefolius*) can be found* (opposite left). *Moss drapes the trees in the 'cloud forests' of Mount Kinabalu* (above) *which start around 1,950 metres (6,400 feet) up on the Summit Trail. In this region of almost permanent cloud, the damp atmosphere creates a fairyland of delicate mosses, ferns and orchids* (opposite middle). *At 3,300 metres (11,000 feet) compact, shrubby species such as* Rhododendron ericoides (opposite right) *clothe the slopes. At the highest altitudes, on the great summit plateau* (opposite above), *very little plant life survives. Seen here from Low's Peak, named after Hugh Low who led the first expedition to ascend the summit, is Low's Gully, a great chasm which falls almost vertically for over 1,000 metres (3,300 feet). Although mountaineering skills are not needed for the Summit Trail, Mount Kinabalu still presents a challenge to explorers: five British soldiers were lost in Low's Gully for four weeks in March 1994.*

Above: *In Sabah's interior, across the Crocker Range from Kota Kinabalu, is the picturesque valley of Tambunan surrounded by terraced rice paddies. In the hills around the town are groves of bamboo which provide the raw materials for fences, traditional homes made of split bamboo and even backpacks for carrying firewood. Tambunan's most famous son, the renowned warrior Mat Salleh, who led an uprising against the British, is buried in the valley.* Opposite: *In the far south-east of Sabah the Segama River flows through the Danum Valley, where a field studies centre has been set up by the Sabah Foundation to document the rich animal and plant life of the reserve's lowland rainforest.* Above left: Trichosanthes *species;* left: Baccaurea *species;* above: Cookeina tricholoma.

*Semporna on Sabah's south-east coast is renowned for the Bajau, once known as Sea Gypsies, who make up the bulk of its population, and for its fresh seafood. Its lively market is set up on piers jutting out over the water* (above). *Picturesque groves of coconut palms line the unspoilt east coast of Sabah and its offshore islands* (left).

Opposite above: *One of the many small islands dotting the waters off Semporna, some the remnants of ancient volcanic craters, which are reputed to offer the best scuba-diving in Malaysia. Turtles come to these islands to nest.*

Opposite below: *Pulau Sipadan is Malaysia's only oceanic island, some three hours' journey by boat from Semporna in the Celebes Sea. The reef comes right up to the beach by the island's small pier, and its coral gardens, caverns and underwater passages make it one of the world's most exciting dive-sites.*

CK KIM HIN
鉄 廠
FOUNDRY

# The People

Dressed in silky gowns the colours of tropical flowers, a trio of Malay women barter for fish in the market. Alongside, an Indian matron swathed in a sari haggles with the fishmonger over a fish head for today's curry, and next to her a couple of Chinese grandmothers in clogs inspect the day's catch. Nearby, a tall Sikh girl with waist-length braids chats with her Eurasian neighbour, whose striking Iberian features attest to her Portuguese ancestry. The market is in Georgetown, Penang, but it could just as well be in a score of other Malaysian towns, for no other Asian land can lay claim to such a diverse population.

Geography has everything to do with it. Located on the great trade route between India and China, the nation has played host to international travellers for thousands of years. Trade, immigration, shifting settlements, religion and colonialism have all played a part in creating Malaysia's rich cultural fabric.

Despite the acceptance of Bahasa Malayu (Malay) as the official language, English, Chinese and Indian dialects are commonly used in towns, and aboriginal languages are still cherished by the Orang Asli and original Bornean peoples.

On the Peninsula, the Malays are the dominant group, with those of Chinese ancestry numbering one third, Indians around ten per cent, and the rest composed of various Orang Asli groups and other small minorities like the Eurasians. In East Malaysia, the Malay and Muslim peoples of the coastal regions comprise around two-thirds of the population, while the Chinese are prominent in the urban centres. Sarawak's indigenous groups include the Iban, the Bidayuh, the Kayan-Kenyah peoples of the upriver regions, the Kelabit of the central highlands and the nomadic Penan. Sabah's major ethnic peoples are the Kadazan, who live in the shadow of the mighty Mount Kinabalu, and the related Dusun and Murut groups.

*Orang Asli, which means 'original people', is the term used to describe some twenty groups of indigenous aboriginals throughout Peninsular Malaysia. A man from the Batek tribe* (left)*, a sub-group of the Semang, demonstrates the use of a blow-pipe in hunting for squirrels in Taman Negara. Although some Batek are still nomadic, most live in settlements close to the forest where they still have the option to hunt and gather fruit like the durian, which is said to taste best when plucked from the wild* (above).

Previous pages
Page 102. Above left: *An Orang Asli girl from central Peninsular Malaysia.*
Above right: *Sitting at the window of her Penang shophouse, a Chinese woman makes an early morning offering.*
Below left: *An elderly Malay woman takes a rest on the steps of her ancestral home at Merlimau, south of Melaka, the vivid colours of her batik sarong vying with those of the art nouveau tiles at her feet.*
Below right: *An Iban dancer, decked in a hornbill-feather head-dress, silver jewellery and beads, performs a ceremonial war-dance at a cultural performance in Kuching.*
Page 103. *Elaborately decorated* bangau *boats at Pantai Dasar Sabak, near Kota Bharu, Kelantan.*
Pages 104-5. *Making blowpipe darts at an Orang Asli settlement in Pahang.*

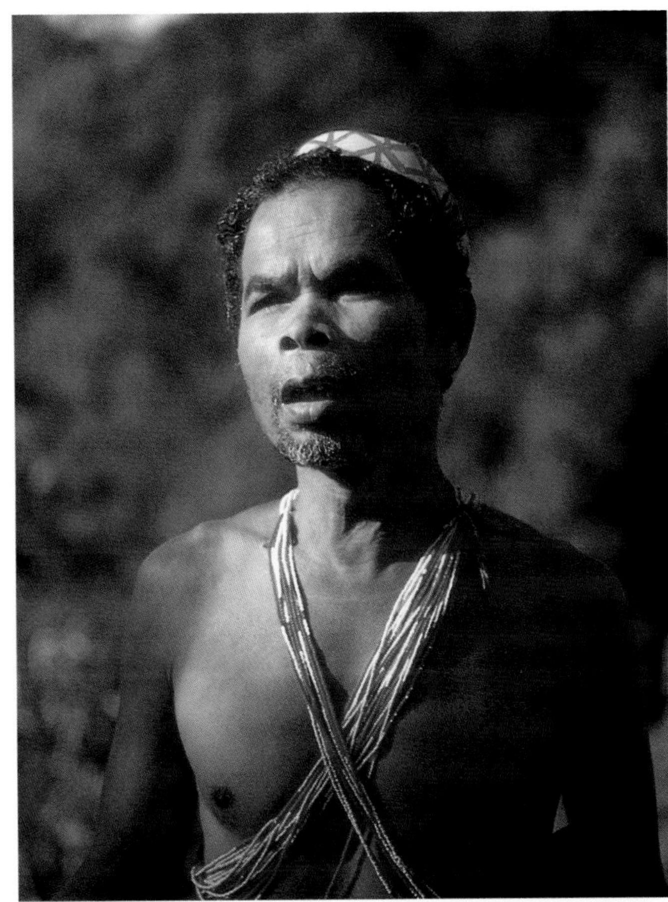

Above: *Pion Anak Bumbon, a master craftsman from the Mah Meri tribe on Carey Island off the coast of Selangor, carries on the tradition of sculpting figures from legendary tales which form part of his rich cultural legacy.*

Above right: *This Senoi tribesman from the Perak highlands, wearing a bark headband and necklaces of trade beads, once practised slash and burn agriculture but he now sells jungle produce to passers-by on the road to Cameron Highlands.*

Right: *The Endau-Rompin region is home to this Orang Asli woman's tribe, known as Orang Ulu or Jakun, who are expert at collecting forest products like camphor, rattan and resins.*

*Malays predominate on the east coast of the Peninsula where fishing is still one of the major occupations.* Above: *Wearing their distinctive regional head-dresses, these men at Pantai Sri Tujuh, near Tumpat in the far north of Kelantan, work as a team to haul in their net while one of them splashes in the shallows to urge the fish into a corner.* Left: *At Beserah, a fishing port in Pahang, fish are still loaded off the boat and onto a bullock-drawn cart in the traditional way, while on the beach women, shaded by large straw hats to protect against the harsh equatorial sun, lay salted fish on a raised drying platform. The village is famous for its* ikan kering *– dried fish – which is a staple food especially during the monsoon when the seas are too rough for the fishermen to work.*

Above: *Idyllic scenes, like this sunset vista of fishing boats at Kedai Buluh on the Kelantan River, are easy to find in this picturesque and unspoiled part of Malaysia.*

Right: *A far busier scene as an abundance of fresh fish arrives at the busy trawler harbour of Kota Kinabalu, the capital of Sabah.*

*Traditional Malay architecture is perfectly in tune with its environment. On the road to Kukup in Johor, the most southerly village in mainland Asia, this delightful house* (opposite above) *features a sunburst pattern on the gable, and a covered entrance foyer which is a feature of Johorean architecture. It is surrounded by coconut palms, fruit trees and herbs which provide food all year round.* Opposite below left: *Set high on stilts to avoid flooding, or even in the past to protect the inhabitants from attacks by tigers, and with long windows open to the breeze, this wooden house in Pulau Langkawi is typical of the styles seen in Kedah. In the fishing villages clustered along the rivers, such as those at Kuala Gula* (opposite below right) *and Kuala Perlis on the Peninsula's west coast* (above), *the wooden houses are erected on platforms jutting out over the water. The traditional roof of* atap, *or Nipa palm thatch is now more usually replaced with corrugated zinc, though it is less effective as an insulator. Fishing boats tie up beside the houses, which are connected by precarious wooden walkways. The shady verandah* (right) *is an essential feature in every Malay house.*

*Outdoor markets and open-air eating are a way of life in Malaysia, and the huge arrays of fruits and vegetables, as well as a rich variety of different cuisines, make eating not merely a favourite pastime but a passion for Malaysians. For sights, smells and colour, nowhere beats the Central Market in Kota Bharu, Kelantan* (above).

Left: *Said to provide instant energy, sugar cane juice is an invigorating refreshment. At Kuala Perlis, a vendor crushes the cane to extract the juice.*

Below: *Durian season is one of the major highlights of the harvest calendar, especially in Penang where aficionados pay exorbitant prices for the first fruit.*

*Malaysians are great lovers of seafood, and on both sides of the South China Sea there are thousands of restaurants and food-stalls which specialize in crabs, shellfish, lobsters, squid, ray and every type of fish – a cuisine which is known collectively as* makanan laut *– 'food from the sea'.*

Right: *Penangites are justly proud of their cuisine, which is renowned throughout the region. The common wayside hawker stall is often where the best food is found, like this stand in the Lebuh Campbell market where a special type of fried bread is a popular snack mid-morning with coffee.*

*Rice, the staple food of Malaysia, is grown throughout the country, but the major crop is from the plains of the two northern states of Kedah and Perlis, an area known as 'the rice bowl' which produces over fifty per cent of the nation's home-grown rice supplies.* Opposite: *Limestone hills, reminiscent of scenes from Chinese silk paintings, rear from the rice paddies near Chuping in Perlis. High up in the cliffside caves is found the guano – the droppings of cave swiftlets and bats – which provided early farmers with nutrient-rich fertilizer.* Above: *A mechanical rice plough lumbers across a paddy in Perlis.* Right: *On the road to Yan, on the coastal plains of Kedah, women still plant out the rice seedlings by hand, though most of the crop is now harvested by machine.* Below right: *Outside Alor Setar, the capital of Kedah, the roadside is lined with workers bagging the paddy at harvest time.*

Top: *Rubber was first planted in Malaysia by H. N. Ridley, known as 'Mad Ridley' for his fervour, in 1888. It immediately thrived, to the chagrin of his detractors, and by 1908 rubber was planted in every state. By 1913 this crop had bypassed tin as Malaysia's chief export, and it stayed at the top until 1980. Many plantations are huge and are owned by corporations but there are still smallholdings, like the one this man works on Pulau Tioman* (left). *He is shouldering sheets of rubber made by pouring the latex into a mould and pressing it. Trees are still tapped by hand in the early morning and the resulting latex is carried to the factory in buckets* (above).

Above: *Timber is Malaysia's most controversial export and one of the nation's major foreign currency earners. However, recent moves by the government have placed more emphasis on sawn timber, and the export of logs from Peninsular Malaysia has been banned. Reforestation and regeneration programmes are now active and many areas have been set aside as reserves and protected forests.*

Right: *Clambering around the terraced hillsides, this tea-picker in Cameron Highlands is a descendant of the first workers shipped from India and Sri Lanka to help with the pioneer plantation which began in the 1930s.*

*Traditional Malay arts and crafts still thrive on Peninsular Malaysia's east coast. Holding aloft his shadow-puppets, this puppet-master from Kelantan* (above left) *not only makes and paints his puppets, but manipulates and provides the voices for at least 50 different characters at each show.*

Above: *Government-run craft workshops like this one at Enggor in Perak provide training for young Malaysians interested in learning their traditional crafts. The style known as 'pumpkin pottery', like the gourd-shaped water container this potter is finishing, originates from the nearby village of Sayong.*

Left: *The production of batik textiles by hand-painting wax and dyes onto the cloth is a large cottage industry in the villages around Kota Bharu, where young girls are employed creating sarong lengths to be made into traditional Malay outfits, and to sell to tourists.*

Above: *Resplendent in their rainbow hues, these decorated craft known as* 'bangau boats' *from their spar-holders which resemble the* bangau *or egret, are a distinctive feature of the fishing village of Kampung Dasar Sabak in the north of Kelantan.*

Below: *Traditionally played at harvest time, giant drums known as* rebana ubi *are now a central part of the entertainment at all Kelantan festivals, and there is even an annual contest when participants from all over the state fill the air with their thunderous drumming.*

FOLLOWING PAGES
*Dressed in purdah, the Arabic veil favoured by only a very small minority of Islamic fundamentalists in Malaysia, this woman and her child take a rest on the cool marble floor of the Masjid Jamek, Kuala Lumpur's original city mosque, built at the confluence of the Kelang and Gombak rivers.*

*Although all Malaysians are allowed freedom to follow the faith of their choice, Islam is the official religion. All Malays, some Indians and some indigenous East Malaysians are Muslims, and the strength of the religion is evident from the number of mosques found throughout the nation.* Above: *With its distinctive onion-shaped dome gleaming in the sun, the Masjid Ubudiah at Kuala Kangsar, the royal capital of Perak, is one of the nation's most renowned mosques. In its cool, marble interior* (left), *worshippers face the Kiblat at Mecca to join in the midday prayers. Construction began in 1913 but was delayed when new marble had to be ordered from Italy after one of the Sultan's bull elephants ran amok while in rut, destroying the first shipment.*

Opposite: *Malay women, dressed modestly in line with Koranic teachings, wear their traditional outfits known as* baju kurung *while waiting for a bus in Kuala Lumpur's Jalan Tuanku Abdul Rahman, the city's best bargain shopping thoroughfare, named after the first prime minister of Malaysia.*

*Many Malaysian Chinese, who form around 37 per cent of the nation's population, follow their traditional religions like Buddhism, Taoism and Confucianism, and their temples are a colourful part of the scenery in both Peninsular and East Malaysia. The Kek Lok Si Temple* (opposite), *outside Ayer Hitam on Penang, is the largest temple complex in South-east Asia and is crowned by the '10,000 Buddhas Precious Pagoda'. The temple was constructed between 1890 and 1910 and was inspired by a Buddhist abbot's vision when he saw that the surrounding hills resembled a crane – the Buddhist symbol of immortality.*

Above and right: *Malaysia's most elaborate clan-house, the Khoo Kongsi in Georgetown, has beautiful gilding, carvings and paintings, and the huge tiled roof, reputed to weigh 25 tons, has ceramic sculptures decorating its upturned roof ridges. This clan-house was built after another even more sumptuous forerunner was burnt to the ground in 1898, an act which was attributed to the gods' annoyance that mere mortals had built something so lavish in honour of their ancestors.*

Above: *Lebuh Chulia, one of the oldest streets in Georgetown, Penang, has a distinctive Chinese flavour like many downtown areas of Malaysia. The English colonials encouraged Chinese immigrants to set up businesses here and as a result their presence is significant even today.*

Left: *Open-fronted shops, like this grocery stall in Georgetown which stocks an amazing variety of essentials, are a characteristic scene in all Malaysian towns and cities.*

Above and right: *In Kuala Lumpur's Central Market, where artists and craftspeople are encouraged to set up shop, a Chinese artist perpetuates the style of his ancestors, and outside the Thean Hou Temple two lion dancers celebrate a Chinese festival.*

Below: *A sea of colourful umbrellas crowd the street on Kuala Lumpur's Jalan Petaling, the capital's favourite market, in the heart of Chinatown.*

Above left: *A flight of 272 steps must be climbed to reach the Batu Caves, a series of limestone caverns high in a cliff on the outskirts of Kuala Lumpur. Inside the cavernous Temple Cave, hung with spectacular stalactites, is a century-old shrine sacred to Malaysia's Hindus* (left). *Every year at Thaipusam, a festival in honour of the deity Vishnu is held when upwards of 100,000 pilgrims, some pierced with spikes in penance for past sins, make the arduous climb to the top.* Top: *One of the resident macaques, amongst many animals given sanctuary at the caves, waits on the stairway to be fed by a passing visitor.* Above: *A statue of Vishnu at the cave entrance.*

*The Bujang Valley in Kedah is one of the richest archaeological sites in Malaysia. Some 50* candi *(temples) have been found here, relics of an early Hindu civilization dating back to the fifth century. The Candi* Bukit Batu Pahat (above) *is the most important of these structures. The arrival of Islam in the 14th century saw the end of this civilization, but its influence on Malay life was far-reaching.*

Right: *Surrounded by curry spices and all the essentials for Indian cuisine, this Melakan storekeeper is a member of Malaysia's Indian population numbering around 10 per cent of the country's total. Indian traders first came to Melaka in the 15th century when the port was known as the 'Queen of the Spice Trade'. However, most Indian Malaysians today are descendants of the contract workers who were shipped from the sub-continent to work in the rubber and copra estates during the British colonial era.*

*Notorious a century ago for their prowess at head-hunting, the Iban are the most numerous of all Sarawak's ethnic peoples. They originally came from Kalimantan where many related groups still live. Although many Iban now live in towns, longhouses like this one on the banks of the Rajang River* (opposite) *are still the favoured residence of country dwellers. These communal buildings may contain between 10 and 50 families, who each live in a separate apartment known as a* bilik, *but much of the work is done on the* tanju, *a long verandah which runs the length of the longhouse.*

*Elaborate beaded costumes and heirloom jewellery are brought out only for festive occasions* (above right and right). Above left: *A group of Iban children in their everyday shorts and T-shirts at the Pyot longhouse near Barudi on the Baram River.*

*In the middle of the Plain of Bah, enclosed by mountains in the highlands of Sarawak, is Bario, the home of the Kelabit people. Although similar to the Kayan and Kenyah peoples, the Kelabit prefer to live in the remote uplands, have more sophisticated methods of irrigation and rice cultivation, and alone of the Borneo peoples their ancestors carved megaliths and dolmens.* Opposite and right: *These days only elderly Kelabit still sport distinctive stretched earlobes hung with brass weights. In infancy their ears were pierced with a thorn and were extended by increasingly heavy metal earrings.* Below: *This Kelabit man combines his western jacket and jeans with a cap decorated with hornbill feathers and the teeth of the Clouded Leopard.*

*Other than trekking overland, the only way to get to Bario is by Malaysian Airlines, which fly Twin Otter planes from Miri and Marudi. The spectacular countryside of the highlands is becoming popular with backpackers and many of the valley longhouses accept overnight guests.*

*The Penan are the only true nomads of Sarawak and traditionally they spent their entire lives deep in the rainforest, hunting and gathering food and produce, living in temporary shelters, and then moving on when game became scarce. They are the people most affected by logging and the government is now encouraging them to lead a more settled existence. These children (above), at a government-run settlement near Gunung Mulu National Park, will probably adapt to their new life, but for older people like the headman and his wife (left) the changes are more traumatic and many bemoan the loss of their old ways.*

Right: *The Illanun, once feared as pirates, grow rice and raise cattle and horses on the open grassland of the Tempasuk Plain in western Sabah. This house is constructed from poles and Nipa palm thatch.*

*Kota Belud, in the north-west of Sabah, is famed for its weekly* tamu, *a lively market complete with a unique water-buffalo auction which is held every Sunday morning. The buffalo are raised by the local Bajau, nicknamed 'the cowboys of the east'. The men congregate for the auction* (below), *while the women, clad in batik and chewing on betel-nut, sell their wares under a canopy of gaily coloured awnings* (following pages).

# THE WILDLIFE

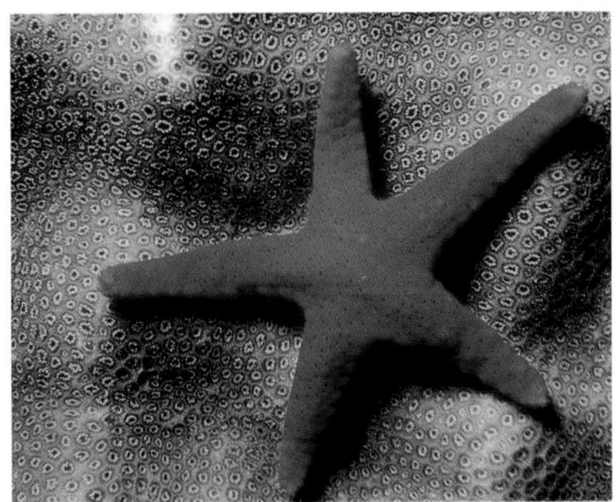

Bird-eating spiders, fish that climb trees, snakes that can fly, and other wondrous oddities like the decidedly humanoid Orang-utan and the minuscule Mouse-deer, have served to fascinate the reading public ever since Malaysia's wildlife was first written about in 18th-century journals. Although they dwelt on the weird and wonderful, they also illustrated the enormous diversity of Malaysia's animal life. This lush country is home to almost 200 species of mammals, over 600 bird species in Peninsular Malaysia alone, 200 different snakes and lizards, over 1,000 butterfly species, 8,000 moth species and insects so numerous that no one is yet prepared to give an estimate.

The rainforest is adept at camouflaging its inhabitants. The larger animals like tigers, leopards, elephants and wild oxen, masters of disguise and stealth, have always stayed deep in the forest. The unique Tapir, sometimes seen in Taman Negara, blends perfectly in a moonlit rainforest, while the Sumatran Rhino – the world's most endangered animal – is rarely seen even by naturalists. The unmistakable whooping cries of the gibbons which reverberate around the montane forests are familiar to forest trekkers, but the animals are less easily seen than heard.

The forest is paradise for bird-watchers, however. Hornbills glide above the canopy, sunbirds and flower-peckers flash their gorgeous hues, while pheasants and pittas peck about on the forest floor.

Malaysian fish include the Giant Catfish which, legend has it, can mesmerize monkeys, and the mud-skippers which waddle about the mangrove and mud flats on modified pectoral fins. Reptiles range from crocodiles to tiny frogs. Giant Leatherback Turtles still come ashore in Terengganu to breed every year, and the coral reefs are home to a huge variety of marine life.

Previous pages

Page 138. Above left: *The rare Argus Pheasant* (Argusianus argus), *one of Malaysia's most spectacular birds. The male has magnificent, metre-long tail feathers, which he uses in elaborate courtship displays.*

Above right: *At the Sepilok Sanctuary in Sabah, Orang-utan* (Pongo pygmaeus) *which have been captive or injured are rehabilitated and taught to return to their native habitat.*

Below left: *The Slow Loris* (Nycticebus coucang), *a frequent nocturnal visitor to rural gardens and plantations throughout Malaysia.*

Below right: *A shoal of Gold-lined Sea Bream* (Gnathodentex aureolineatus) *shimmer in the sparkling waters around Pulau Sipadan off the coast of Sabah.*

Page 139: *A startlingly coloured starfish resting on coral off Kota Kinabalu.*

OPPOSITE PAGE

Top: *A mother elephant* (Elephas maximus) *and her calf. The habitat of Malaysian elephants has been greatly disturbed by agricultural clearance, but some have now been moved to protected forests by the government-run elephant relocation unit.*

Bottom: *Wallowing in a mud-bath in the Dusun Forest Reserve, this Sumatran Rhinoceros* (Dicerorhinus sumatrensis) *is one of Malaysia's rarest herbivores, and is said to be the world's most endangered animal.*

Top right: *Known as* seladang, *wild oxen* (Bos gaurus) *like this bull in a captive breeding herd can weigh up to 1,500 kilograms (1.5 tons) and are the largest of the world's wild oxen.*

Right: *Wild pigs* (Sus scrofa) *are one of the easiest of all Malaysian animals to spot and have even been seen running across the highway in the suburbs of Kuala Lumpur.*

Below: *Said to be still evolving, the herbivorous Tapir* (Tapirus indicus) *bears a slight resemblance to a pig, but it has a trunk-like nose. Not found in Sabah or Sarawak, the largest population in Peninsular Malaysia is probably in Taman Negara.*

Above: *The Greater Mouse-deer* (Tragulus napu) *is the larger of the two species of mouse-deer found in Malaysia, quite common in the lowland forests, but shy and difficult to spot. They are most active at night.*

Left: *Standing only 50 centimetres (20 inches) high at the shoulder, Barking Deer* (Muntiacus muntjak), *or* kijang, *named because of their hoarse barking call, are hard to see as they prefer to live in thick forest.*

Below: *Ranging from India to Sulawesi, the Sambar Deer, or* rusa (Cervus unicolor), *stands from 1 to 1.5 metres (3 to 5 feet) tall. They have a habit of stamping their feet when they suspect they are in danger, a regular occurrence as their venison is prized by hunters.*

Above: *A young Leopard Cat* (Felis bengalensis). *Found from India to Indonesia, the Leopard Cat is not fussy when it comes to habitat, living in forest, plantation areas and even in the suburbs.*

Right: *Once found from Siberia to Iran and as far south as Sumatra, the Tiger* (Felis tigris) *is now one of the world's most endangered species. Measuring around 2.5 metres (8 feet) in length and weighing up to 225 kilograms (500 lb), it is no wonder that the Malayan Tiger has always been known as the king of the forest. Beautifully camouflaged and with excellent sensory powers, they are difficult to spot amongst the trees, but their footprints can sometimes be seen in Endau-Rompin and Taman Negara, especially in areas where wild pigs, their favoured food, have been digging for roots.*

Bottom right: *The most attractively marked of all the Malaysian cats, the Clouded Leopard* (Neofelis nebulosa) *is not quite as large as the Panther or Tiger, but is still sizeable, measuring up to 2 metres (6 feet) long. Preferring to live in forests where it spends most of its time in the trees, its Malay name of* rimau dahan *is apt – 'tiger of the tree branches'.*

*Although the name 'Orang-utan' means 'man of the forest' in Malay, this name was coined by Europeans as the Malays know them as* mawas. *Native only to Sumatra and Borneo,* Pongo pygmaeus, *the largest ape found outside Africa, lives to around 40 years of age and has about the same body size as a man. The young are weaned when they are two, becoming mature at eight, but as they are dependent on their mothers until they are five, young Orang-utan which are released into the forest will die if they have not been taught the necessary skills to survive. At Sabah's Sepilok Rehabilitation Centre, where these photographs were taken, apes which have been confiscated from captivity or brought in from logging camps are reconditioned and taught how to survive in the wild. The centre was set up in the 1960s and since then over 200 Orang-utan have been successfully re-integrated into their original habitat.* Opposite: *Mature male.* Above: *Mother and child.* Above right: *Orang-utan on its sleeping nest of branches in the forest canopy.* Right: *Two-year-old.*

Above left: *Long-tailed Macaques* (Macaca fascicularis), *like this one grooming her young in Penang, are numerous and widespread throughout South-east Asia. Because they occasionally hunt crabs they have sometimes been called Crab-eating Macaques, but they have indiscriminate food habits, and because of their boldness they often pester householders and picnickers, especially in Penang's Botanical Gardens where feeding them is forbidden.*

*Even casual visitors to the Malaysian rainforest usually notice the distinctive hoots of the gibbons as they swing with wonderful agility through the trees. Known in Malay as* wak-wak, *pronounced 'wah wah', this name accurately describes the gibbons' musical voices. All gibbons are mainly vegetarian but they also have a taste for certain insects. The White-handed Gibbon* (Hylobates lar) *has characteristic white feet and hands, though the rest of its body varies in colour from pale cream* (opposite) *to black* (above). *It is found in Peninsular Malaysia while* (left) *the Bornean Gibbon* (Hylobates muelleri) *is found only in Borneo.*

Above: *The nature reserve at Kuala Selangor is the best place for visitors to spot the attractive Silvered Leaf Monkeys* (Presbytis cristata) *with their contrasting orange-coloured young. Leaf monkeys are strict vegetarians and they use their long tails, which are one and a half times their body length, to swing effortlessly through the forest.*

Left: *A young Dusky Leaf Monkey on Pulau Langkawi. Also known as a Spectacled Langur because of its white ringed eyes, this particular leaf monkey,* Presbytis obscura, *is found only on the Peninsula, not in Sabah and Sarawak.*

*The strangest of all monkeys is the Proboscis Monkey* (Nasalis larvatus), *which is known by the Malays as* kera belanda, *the 'Dutch monkey', because of its large bulbous nose, a facial characteristic apparently once prominent amongst Dutch colonials in Kalimantan. The nose is large and drooping on the males* (right) *but is short and pert on females and young, and its purpose is unknown, although it is used when the males make their peculiar honking sound. The Proboscis Monkey is found only in the coastal swamps of Borneo and it lives almost exclusively on the leaves of the* Sonneratia *tree.*

Above: *Sabah's Danum Valley is home to this Malay Civet* (Viverra tangalunga). *Resembling a cat, but actually a primitive member of the Carnivora, it lives on the ground and its diet includes small reptiles and insects. The Malay Civet differs from other species by its unusual tail markings of ten black and white rings which are joined by a black stripe.*

Above left: *The nocturnal Slow Loris* (Nycticebus coucang) *lives on insects and small lizards, but it is also fond of fruit. It moves slowly along tree limbs, but it can be surprisingly fast at catching prey. Its Malay name,* kongkang, *is also used to mean 'to bite', like a dog's bite, which implies that it is not as cuddly as its appearance would indicate.*

Left: *Known in Malay as the* beruang, *the Malayan Sun Bear* (Helarctos malayanus) *feeds on wild honey, fruits, termites and occasionally small invertebrates. It may stand only 1.5 metres (5 feet) tall, but it is aggressive if it feels threatened, especially when near its den. In spite of its fiery temper, however, Sir Stamford Raffles kept a Sun Bear as a pet and allowed it to share his dinner-table, where it apparently insisted on a diet of mangosteens and champagne.*

Opposite, top: *Often to be seen around the trails of Kinabalu Park, the Mountain Treeshrew* (Tupaia montana) *is the commonest mammal in this area, though it is not found elsewhere in Malaysia.*

Above: *A Small-clawed Otter* (Amblonyx cinerea) *feasting on fish on the bank of a forest stream in Sabah.*

Right: *One of a large number of 'flying' mammals in the Malaysian rainforests, the Colugo or Flying Lemur* (Cynocephalus variegatus) *is the most unusual, not closely related to any other species. Membranes link its limbs and tail, making an effective parachute which allows it to glide as far as 100 metres (330 feet) between trees.*

Opposite: *The Great Hornbill* (Buceros bicornis), *a member of Malaysia's most spectacular family of birds. With their harsh cries and noisy flight, the bizarre hornbills, named because of their huge hollow casques, are easy to spot as they fly across the rainforests throughout the country. The largest species* (below right) *is the Rhinoceros Hornbill* (Buceros rhinoceros), *which gets its name from its large red-and-yellow casque curving upwards at the front. The Wreathed Hornbill* (Rhyticeros undulatus) *frequents forested hills. Like all hornbills, the male of the species* (right) *has the curious habit of walling the female* (below) *into her nest during the incubation period. He feeds her through a small hole and then when the young bird is mature enough to fly he pecks the wall away.*

Above left: *In the mangrove forests of the Perak coast, the Kuala Gula Bird Sanctuary provides a protected home for the rare Milky Storks* (Mycteria cinerea) *which have a strange habit of fishing in ponds with their bills half open.*

Above: *The Lesser Adjutant Stork* (Leptoptilos javanicus) *stands at 45cm (18 inches) tall and is found from Sri Lanka to Malaysia. Because of its bald head, the Malays call it* burung botak, *'bald-headed bird'.*

Left: *The Black-crowned Night Heron* (Nycticorax nycticorax) *lives mainly on fish but it often varies its diet with insects and small rodents, setting out at dusk to hunt in paddy fields and swamps. This is an immature bird.*

Opposite: *With its large, bright red bill, white bib and rufous head, the White-throated Kingfisher* (Halcyon smyrnensis) *differs from other species by preferring a diet of lizards and frogs to the regular kingfisher fare of fish.*

*The noisy and brilliantly coloured Eastern Green Magpie* (Cissa chinensis) *has a range that extends from Borneo up to the Himalayas.*

Above: *The shy Crested Wood Partridge* (Rollulus roulroul) *inhabits the lowland forest floor, foraging for insects and fallen fruits. This is the female bird, whose subtly coloured feathers serve as efficient camouflage on the ground. The male boasts a striking reddish-brown crest.*

Below: *Mountain forests are home to the exuberant laughing thrushes, such as this White-crested Laughing Thrush* (Garrulax leucolophus), *who wander through the forest in troops, performing acrobatics in loops of creeper and uttering loud musical calls.*

Above: *Red-wattled Lapwings* (Lobivanellus indicus) *are restless, lively, wading birds, calling loudly during their breeding season.*

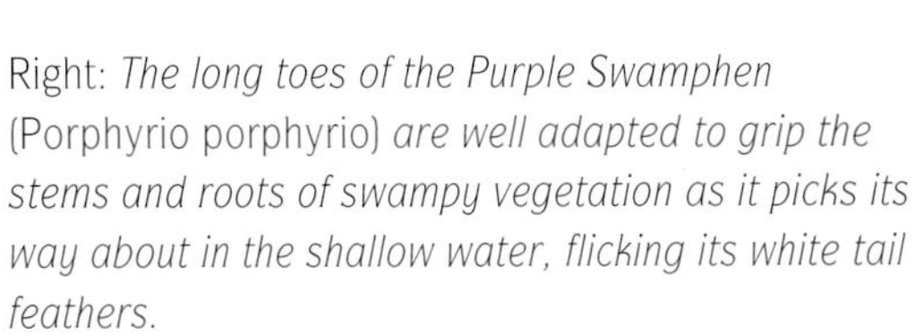

Right: *The long toes of the Purple Swamphen* (Porphyrio porphyrio) *are well adapted to grip the stems and roots of swampy vegetation as it picks its way about in the shallow water, flicking its white tail feathers.*

Left: Papilio demoleus malayanus, *commonly known as the Lime Butterfly. Its black and yellow patterned wings can often be spotted as a splash of colour in the sombre rainforest.*

Above: *A Golden Birdwing* (Troides amphrysus ruficollis), *a splendid member of this striking group of butterflies.*

Opposite, above: *The Malaysian rainforest probably has more butterflies per hectare than anywhere else on the planet, and the most spectacular must be the Rajah Brooke's Birdwing* (Troides brookiana), *with its velvety black and brilliant green forewings and a wingspan of up to 18 centimetres (7 inches). It was discovered by the famous naturalist Alfred Russel Wallace and named after the 'White Rajah' of Sarawak.*

Above right: *The Plain Tiger butterfly* (Danaus chrysippus alcippoides), *named for its orange and black striped markings, is a common sight on the plains and in villages, but it is not found in the forest.*

Right: *The elegant Smaller Wood Nymph* (Ideopsis gaura perakana) *has a distinctive slow manner of flying.*

Below: Graphium *species on a river-bank in Taman Negara. Butterflies, almost always males, are often seen gathered on the shores of streams in the rainforest where they apparently suck the wet sand, attracted by the urine deposits of animals.*

*So great are the numbers of insect species throughout Malaysia that their total is still to be assessed, and new species are constantly being discovered. Camouflaged by the detritus of the forest floor* (above left), *insects are constantly at work breaking down the leaf litter. Amongst the most underestimated of all the insects are the termites which mainly feed on rotting wood. They are sometimes mistakenly called 'white ants' but they are actually an order of their own, Isoptera, whose closest relative is the cockroach. Their pillar-shaped mounds* (top right), *built on the forest floor, are made with a mixture of masticated wood pulp and saliva.* Top left: *Columns of soldier termites, known for practising chemical warfare when intruders try to enter their nests, move across the forest floor in Taman Negara.*

Above right: Hydnophytum formicarium, *an epiphyte which enjoys a symbiotic relationship with ants. They make their home in the swollen bases of its stems, and in return protect it from caterpillars while their droppings provide the plant with nutrients.*

*Spiders often feature in Malaysian folklore as heroic and helpful creatures, probably because the Prophet Muhammad was once helped by a spider when he wanted to escape from his enemies. There are spiders as small as ants, those so big that they actually feast on birds, and others that do the admirable job of dining off cockroaches.*

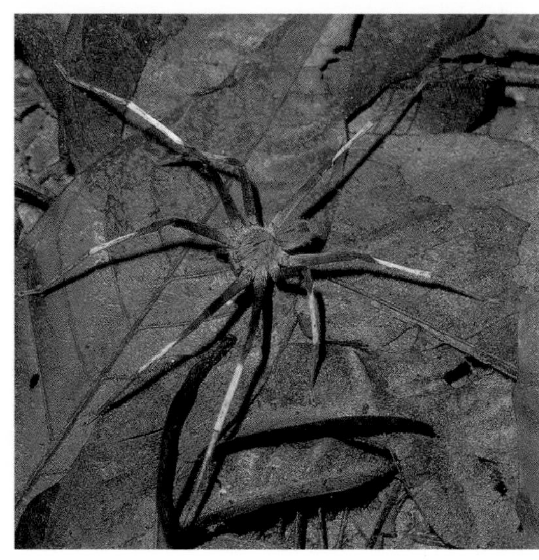

*Gauzy-winged dragonflies are commonly found hovering over ponds, in gardens and by the roadside all over Malaysia. The young nymphs first live in the water breathing with gills, then when they are mature they climb onto a reed where their skin breaks apart and they emerge as an adult dragonfly.* Above: Neurothemis terminata. Left: Orthetrum glaucum.

Right: *The Flower Mantis,* (Hymenopus coronatus), *often described as the most remarkable of Malaysian insects, has the uncanny ability to turn itself into a 'flower'. As an adult during its winged phase it looks like an ordinary white mantis except for the petal-like protuberances on its thigh joints. However, in its unwinged phase, it changes colour to a bright pink, its hind part arches over its back, and its petal-like thighs give it the appearance of an orchid. Its prey are lured into thinking that this fierce predator is actually a harmless flower. Other insects with remarkable camouflage include* (below left) *the Moving Leaf Insect* (Phyllicum giganteum) *and* (below right) *the Giant Thorny Stick Insect* (Heteropteryx dilata). *These creatures are harmless and their disguise is for protection.*

Above: *Over a hundred different species of land snake make their home in Malaysia, including this Striped Bronze Back* (Dendrelaphis caudolineatus), *which grows to almost 2 metres (6 feet) in length. It makes its home in trees and feeds on small lizards and frogs.*

Left: *Formerly relentlessly exploited for their skins which are still prized for making luxury handbags, boots and belts, crocodiles are not often seen but they are making a comeback on some rivers and have even been spotted near downtown Melaka. In Malay legend, the Estuarine Crocodile* (Crocodylus porosus) *is believed sometimes to be controlled by magicians who can summon them to do their bidding.*

Below left: *A relic of the age of reptiles is the Water Monitor Lizard* (Varanus salvator), *or* biawak, *as it is known in Malay. They grow to over 2 metres (6 feet) and are often seen swimming in rivers. Their favourite food is turtle and crocodile eggs, but as they are scavengers they will eat all kinds of food including household waste, even leftover curries.*

Opposite: *The Malaysian night is often punctuated by the honking and gronking of its amphibians, which are more often heard than seen. This handsomely coloured Malaysian Tree Frog* (Polypedates otilophus) *has circular suckers on its toe tips to help it grip the trunks and branches of smooth-barked trees.*

*Year after year, between May and September, female Leatherback Turtles* (Dermochelys coriacea) *return to their habitual nesting-places and heave themselves up the sand to dig a pit into which they will each lay up to 150 eggs. The beach at Rantau Abang in Terengganu is one of these rare nesting-sites. An artificial hatchery has been set up here by the Malaysian Fisheries Department in an attempt to conserve the declining population of Leatherbacks. The hatchlings* (below left) *are released into the sea, but most fall prey to birds and fish and very few will reach adulthood.*

Opposite: *Other turtle species are also endangered: both the Green Turtle* (Chelonia mydas, above) *and the Hawksbill Turtle* (Eretmochelys imbricata, below) *have been hunted for centuries as a source of meat and tortoiseshell, and their eggs have been collected on a massive scale.*

Above: *The Clownfish* (Amphiprion ocellaris) *lives in the shallows, under the protection of a sea anemone's stinging tentacles. It is defended from stings itself by the mucus covering its skin.*

Left: *Feather-stars, like their relatives the sea-lilies, are attached by a stalk to a rock in the shallows, where they feed on micro-organisms that drift into their entrapping arms. When adult, however, they are also able to disengage themselves and swim to a new location.*

PREVIOUS PAGES
*A shoal of basslets* (Pseudanthias) *swim over the sunlit coral in the shallow waters around Pulau Sipadan.*

*The seas around Malaysia abound in corals, fish, and all kinds of marine riches. Pulau Sipadan lures divers from all over the world to explore its reef wall, falling away to the bed of the Celebes Sea, 600 metres (1970 feet) below. The site has been a marine reserve since 1981.* Right: *A Mollusc* (Phenacovola) *feeding on a gorgonian coral.* Below: *A colony of sea squirts* (Didemnum molle). Below right: *The Two-eyed Lionfish* (Dendrochirus biocellatus).

FOLLOWING PAGE
*Yellow-fin Goat fish* (Mulliodes vanicolensis).

# INDEX

Page numbers in **bold** type refer to illustrations